Books in the series "Crafting your career in academia":

- Writing effective promotion applications (August 2022)
- Publishing in academic journals (November 2022)
- Creating social media profiles (February 2023)
- Measuring and improving research impact (May 2023)
- Using the Publish or Perish software (August 2023)

Writing effective promotion applications

Crafting your career in academia

Anne-Wil Harzing

Edition: August 2022

ISBN 978-1-7396097-3-3 (paperback, black & white)

Published by Tarma Software Research Ltd, UK

Author	Harzing, Anne-Wil
Title	Writing Effective Promotion Applications. Crafting your career in academia / Anne-Wil Harzing
Edition	1st ed.
ISBN	978-1-7396097-3-3 (paperback, black & white)
Subjects	Academic careers, promotion, academic development
Dewey Number	650.14

Table of contents

Introduction: Why is promotion so important for academics?

Promotion through the academic ranks can be a slow, frustrating, and opaque process and there are few things in academic life which elicit such strong emotions. At the same time, for many academics achieving promotion to full or associate professor is one of the most important milestones of their academic careers.

This is not entirely surprising. Academic salaries are relatively low when compared to other professions that require the same length of training and working hours. Moreover, rejection is a constant feature of academic lives. Hence, promotion is one of the few big positive reinforcements we get in our academic careers.

Even so, there doesn't appear to be a lot of guidance for academics going up for promotion. As a result, many promotion applications are not as effective as they could be. In this book, I have documented the lessons I have learned about applying for promotion, both from a personal and from an institutional perspective, and have provided detailed recommendations for successful promotion applications.

I hope this will help you to better understand the background to this highly contested topic and provide you with the tools to be successful in your own promotion application. I would love to hear from you if you feel this book has helped you; feel free to get in touch with me at anne@harzing.com.

Note: This book is an edited and curated collection of my blogposts on the topic of promotion applications, drawing on my 4-part blogpost series on internal vs. external promotions, published in 2018, and my 6-part blogpost series with practical promotion tips, published in 2022.

Chapter 1: Academic promotion - Understand the process

This first chapter helps you understand the background to academic promotions. It explains why universities promote academics and how you can start to develop a successful promotion application.

A few caveats before we start

These five caveats might help you understand what this book can and can't offer you.

1. My experience is in Australian and British university systems. Other university systems might have different expectations. Even in other countries, however, these tips might still be useful for other purposes such as Fellowship or Award nominations.

2. This book focuses on the most common academic career path: teaching & research. My reflections on teaching/research impact will also be relevant for teaching-only/research-only academics.

3. My tips focus on internal promotions. As argued in Chapter 7, internal promotions often require more justification than external promotions. However, many of my tips are also relevant for external promotions, if not for the job application, then certainly for the presentation and interview.

4. This book is *descriptive*, helping you understand why promotion can be difficult to achieve, and what you can do to improve your chances. It doesn't mean I consider promotion hurdles morally just. But my moral outrage isn't going to get you promoted.

5. My write-up doesn't dwell on bias in universities, or the effect of bias on promotion decisions. Unfortunately, I cannot wave a magic wand to make these biases disappear. What I *can* do, however, is help you to make the best possible case.

Understand *why* universities
promote academics

As in any situation in life, trying to understand your counterpart will lead to a more positive outcome. You don't need to *agree* with the rationales of those on your promotion panel, but you will be much more successful if you *understand* them. I will explore this further in Chapter 7, discussing how incentive structures differ between internal and external promotion.

It is not uncommon for academics to feel that the university "owes" them promotion after a certain number of years of employment. But remember, you are not promoted to reward you for being a loyal servant. Promotions generally reflect the *potential* of what you *can* do in the *future*, they are not a *reward* for what you *have* done in the *past*.

So yes, you *should* use your past achievements to evidence why you should be promoted. But few universities will promote you unless they feel that these past achievements are *indicators* of even bigger future achievements. What you really want to convey to your employer is that promotion would benefit both you *and* the institution, because it would allow you to spread your wings and fly even higher.

Professorial promotions

These reflections are true for promotion to *any* level, but there is an additional "complication" for promotion to full professor. After you reach this top level of the academic hierarchy, the university has less "leverage" over you, i.e., they can't ask you to do jobs because they "will look good for promotion".

Hence, promotion panels might have two concerns. Unless there are clear signals to the contrary, they may fear that you will:

1. Become research inactive. In fact, many professors become more, not less, research-active after promotion; they are intrinsically interested in research and keen to use their new position to do more. But there are also professors who gradually become less and less research active. Their research motivation might well have been a bit more extrinsic, i.e., driven at least partly by career goals. As the university doesn't know which category you belong to, they will be looking for signals of likely future research performance.

2. Start focusing only on your own research interests. As a result, you might be less likely to *actively* engage in teaching or leadership. Many universities rely on professors to do the bulk of academic leadership. Therefore, they are looking for signals that you will be likely to take on these roles, whether they are formal – e.g., as Head of Department or (Associate) Dean – or informal – e.g., through research mentoring or service to the profession.

Start early and create a "good stuff" file

The first step towards a successful promotion application is to start early. Don't wait until the call for promotion applications comes around. That may give you merely a few weeks in which to "throw an application together". This will almost certainly lead to an underdeveloped attempt.

Start thinking about your (next) promotion as soon as you are being appointed (promoted). This will not only provide you with a clearer focus about the type of activities you will need to engage in, but it also gives you time to assemble a good case. Then start drafting an actual application 6-12 months before you submit it.

Second, start a "good stuff" file. This is a file with your professional achievements. Ideally, you should do this at the start of your academic career. However, you should absolutely create one once you start thinking about your promotion application, even if that is years before you apply.

I suggest you create a Word document or a folder for your promotion application today and put it on your desktop. Then simply drop every tiny bit of good news and achievement in it. Getting a nice email from a student or colleague? Take a screenshot and drop it in there. Getting nominated for an award? Put it in there, even if you were not selected. Saw your work cited by a famous academic? Again, take a screenshot and drop it in there.

Don't worry about nice formatting or systematic reporting. Your first aim is simply to gather material in the quickest way possible. If you have half an hour to spare occasionally, you can go through your file and clean it up a bit. Some achievements might go straight to your CV, others might be collated under a specific heading, e.g., evidence of research or teaching impact, or evidence of academic reputation.

Your "good stuff" file will serve at least three purposes. It will:

1. Give you something to start with for your first application draft. There is nothing worse than a blank sheet of paper and a daunting list of promotion criteria.

2. Ensure you don't forget the many small things that in themselves are not consequential but combined might make a strong case. We all think we will remember things when the time comes. We rarely do...

3. Make you feel good about yourself for two reasons. First, you progress your promotion a little bit every day/week/month. Second, you document your achievements, and can look back on them on "dark days".

Diversity of academic career paths

Not every university is the same. Therefore, you might need to tailor your submission. Academic career paths can also vary substantially *between* academics (see also my blogpost "*CYGNA: One size doesn't fit all - Diversity of academic career paths*").

I was therefore particularly pleased to see Middlesex University's new 2022 promotion guidelines acknowledge this explicitly. Rather than presenting applicants with a list of tick-boxes and hurdles, it provides them with the opportunity to make a case based on their unique circumstances.

We recognise that in a complex organisation, people have different career trajectories, and these guidelines provide an indicative framework within which robust qualitative judgements of overall performance can be made.

A new application form has been designed to allow you to reflect on your journey so far. This may include reflection on your achievements prior to joining the University. If this is the case, it is important that in doing so you make clear how you have built upon these achievements in your subsequent work at Middlesex, to benefit the experience of our learners, our research and KE outputs and impact, and the reputation of the University.

The application asks you to articulate what you see to be your areas of strength and also areas you feel you need to develop. If there is a specific area you feel you have not been able to achieve to the expected level, for example you have not seen a doctoral student through to completion, or you have not been awarded a substantive competitive research grant, and there are specific reasons for this, please present these in the application.

Quick preview:

what makes a successful application?

Successful promotion applications *make a case* for promotion. This means *evidencing* that your research, teaching, and leadership has *made a difference*, and embedding this evidence in an overall career narrative. However, many promotion applications that I have seen over the last decades are dry and disjointed summaries, with a simple listing of "*I have done this, this, and this*" without evidence of impact. They lack both a coherent narrative and substantive evidence.

First, rather than relying on dry descriptions or hyperbolic assertions, make a genuine and consistent attempt to evidence your claims. We will look at this in much more detail for the three core aspects of an academic job in the next three chapters: Research & Engagement (Chapter 3), Teaching & Learning (Chapter 4), Leadership & Service (Chapter 5).

Second, create a sense of excitement about what is "on offer" by showing you are not just "ticking the boxes" of the template, but providing a unique contribution. This is what Chapter 6 - Craft your career narrative - is all about.

However, before diving into this, have a look at the second chapter. Here I explain how you can use all the lessons you have learned from submitting your work to journals to get a head-start for your promotion application.

Chapter 2: Treat your application as a journal submission

Hopefully, the first chapter has given you a better understanding of *why* universities (do not) promote academics. Now let's consider the actual process of preparing a promotion application. This process has many similarities with submitting an article for publication. So, why not use all the experience you have gained in this context? Here are ten tips to help you get a head start with your promotion application.

Tip 1: Gather information

Gather as much information as possible, not just about the formal rules (journal guidelines or promotion guidelines), but also about the *informal* rules. For the latter, talking to other academics is essential. Realise though that three anecdotes don't make data. So, listen, but listen critically.

Also realise that academics are more likely to share horror stories (whether about journals or promotions) than positive experiences. They are not different from the general public in that respect. Bad news "sells". And have you noticed that these horror stories somehow tend to get embellished each time they are retold?

Tip 2: Learn by example

In the writing bootcamps I run every year at Middlesex University, I ask participants to find three example papers from the journal they are targeting. I suggest you do the same with promotion applications. However, make sure you select your examples wisely to ensure they provide you with *useful* templates.

First, select examples that are *relevant* to your case. If you submit an article using quantitative methods to a journal, you don't select a qualitative example article. The same principle applies to promotion applications too. Every university has its own promotion guidelines. So, get examples from your own institution. If your colleagues are not willing to share their applications or if there are no recent promotions at your institution, try to find examples from universities with a similar orientation.

Second, get *recent* examples, promotion guidelines may have changed. But more importantly, so have expectations of what performance is needed to get promoted (see the section "the past is another country…" in Chapter 7). You might think that's not fair. I agree. However, it is a reality. Performance criteria do change over time. But so does access to resources: try doing a PhD without access to the internet or even email. Yes, I am that old ☺.

Tip 3: Consider your audience

The way you write up your article or promotion application depends on your audience. You know how this works for journal submissions. Submitting to a specialist journal? You can assume a certain level of familiarity with the main authors, theories, and research methods in the field. Trying your luck in a more highly ranked generalist journal? You might need to provide a bit more justification in all these areas. Writing for a journal in another discipline? You might need to do a *lot* of explaining to get your contribution recognised.

The same is true for promotion applications. Find out who will be deciding on your promotion application. Is it a departmental panel? A panel at the level of your School or Faculty? Or even a university-level panel? Promotion applications for Associate and Full Professor are evaluated at higher organisational levels than applications for promotion to Lecturer or Senior Lecturer. In smaller universities even applications for Associate Professor might be decided at University level. Bigger universities might have separate panels for broader disciplinary areas, such as the Social Sciences, the Sciences, the Life Sciences, Engineering, and the Humanities.

Any promotion application above the departmental level requires *much* more contextualisation, both qualitatively and quantitatively. This is especially true for research. Step outside your own narrow disciplinary area. Remember that beyond *Science* and *Nature* there are very few journals that are recognised across disciplines! The same is true for academic superstars. Are you highlighting your standing in the field through your well-known collaborators? You will find that a famous academic in Marketing might be a complete unknown even in the related discipline of Management.

Are you a Business School academic boasting about publishing three articles a year? Expect to be seen as a slacker in the Life Sciences. Proudly featuring your 50K grant? Academics in the Natural Sciences might wonder why you are even mentioning it. So, include some field benchmarks in your application to contextualise your achievements. I show you how to do this in Chapter 3.

Tip 4: Tailor your submission

We all know we need to tailor our journal articles to the outlet we are submitting our paper to. You wouldn't send a review article to an empirical journal, would you? You are not submitting experimental papers to a journal that focuses on action research. You know only too well that trying to get an article with a student sample published in a Management journal is usually a recipe for failure. So, we learn to pick our journal outlets wisely.

Unfortunately, in internal promotion applications your "outlet" (i.e., university) is fixed. So, if you work at a teaching-intensive university, don't lead with your research performance and vice versa.

If your university values fundamental research, then evidence how your research presented a major advance in the field. Do they care more about societal impact? Ensure you don't just "bang on" about your publications in top journals. By all means mention them, but also explain how your research has made a difference to society.

Is the discrepancy between your academic record and the priorities and the expectations of your university is too large? Then applying externally might well be the only solution if you unable or unwilling to narrow this gap quickly, and you are keen to be promoted. As we discuss in Chapter 7, however, this does bring its own problems.

Tip 5: Realise that packaging does matter

Start early and polish, polish, polish. Yes, content is more important than packaging. But good packaging makes it easier to appreciate the content of your article or promotion application. Just like "normal people" academics are subject to anchoring effects too. The fastest way to annoy an editor/reviewer is to have an abstract with typos or convoluted sentences.

Likewise, I have seen applications that seemed to have been thrown together in a few days. They were full of typos, ungrammatical sentences, and hyperbolic unsupported assertions. This casts serious doubts on your academic abilities. To the promotion panel it might also convey an *"I don't care, and think I am good enough to not bother to spend much time on this"* attitude - which is unlikely to improve your chances of success.

Tip 6: Ask for advice

Get a friendly reader before you submit. You would do this for a journal article wouldn't you? So why not for a promotion application? Be prepared to return a favour though.

For my promotion to Associate Professor, I asked at least half a dozen colleagues, and all said yes. Was that because they were such nice people? Well, they might have been, but more likely it was because I had helped them in the past. Or at least I bought them lunch ☺.

Tip 7: Think R&R, not reject

Treat an unsuccessful application as a revise & resubmit rather than a rejection. Yes, you can go to another journal outlet (university). This might work if that journal's/institution's expectations are entirely different. However, in most cases you will find that unless you take the reviewer comments into account, your submission is unlikely to end happily.

In dealing with a promotion rejection, also try and keep emotions at bay. Well..., at least after a few days of cursing the panel's ignorance and soothing your emotions with wine or chocolate. Most of all though, try not to let it impact on your self-esteem. I know rejections always hurt but do remember this isn't personal. Just address the feedback and try again.

Second, don't withdraw into anger or cynicism over supposed injustice. I certainly feel I have suffered from bias and university politics at several junctures in my career. It has kept me awake at night more than once. Life in academia can be very unfair. But if you focus on this too much, it only makes the effects of it worse. (See also my blog-post *"How to prevent burn-out? About staying sane in academia"*).

Tip 8: Accept you can't control everything

Realise that in journal submissions and promotion applications alike there are always things that are beyond your control. When submitting to journals, success may be dependent on who the acting editor is or whether the journal even has an acting editor with a passing knowledge of the topic of your paper. You are also subject to the "role of the dice" in terms of the academics that accept the invitation to review.

The same is true for promotion applications and promotion panels. Those in university leadership positions of are not the same from one year to another. Hence, promotion panels can vary substantially in composition. Moreover, you cannot control the number and quality of other articles/applications that are submitted at the same time; competition might be stronger in some years or for some journals/-positions than for others.

Capacity might also be larger in some journals and universities than in others. Some journals have expanded the number of articles they publish to match the increasing level of submissions. Others have stuck resolutely to publishing only a small selection of the papers they receive. Likewise, some universities might promote everyone who meets the criteria. Other universities might only have a fixed number of places every year. This means you "compete" with other academics applying at the same time.

Tip 9: Recognise outliers

Just because one article at – what *you think* is – a similar level as yours has been published in a specific journal this doesn't mean that your own article should be. The same is true for promotions.

First, we are all biased. You can rarely compare yourself directly to other academics. We all do when our applications are rejected. "*But I am so much better than so-and-so, I have more …*" What you don't know (or what you conveniently ignore) is that you might well have *much* less of something else. There is more to an academic record than can be gleaned from a 1-minute glance through their list of publications.

Second, standards increase over time. Have a look at what was published in the top journals in your field 20-30 years ago; you might be shocked. The same is true for promotion applications. Have a look at Tip 2 and the section "the past is another country" in Chapter 7 for details.

Third, understand that these articles/individuals might simply have had a "lucky break" or a good "role of the dice". There is absolutely no guarantee you might be equally lucky on your first try. Refer back to Tip 8 for details.

Tip 10: Neutralise academics' critical nature

Remember that as academics we are "programmed" to find faults and reason to reject. That's just the nature of our profession. Every paper submission/ promotion application has its weaknesses, so a panel can *always* find a reason to reject your application.

So, what factors make an editor/reviewer or promotion panel look "beyond" the weaknesses? Two things really. First, rather than rely on hyperbolic assertions, make a genuine and consistent attempt to evidence your claims. We will look at this in much more detail in the next three chapters for each of the three core aspects of academic jobs: Research & Engagement (Chapter 3), Teaching & Learning (Chapter 4), Leadership & Service (Chapter 5).

Second, create a real sense of excitement about what is "on offer" by showing the paper or academic is not just "ticking the boxes" of the template, but providing a unique contribution. This is what the Chapter 6 – Craft your career narrative – is all about.

Chapter 3: Evidence your impact in Research & Engagement

Hopefully the first two chapters – "Understand the process" and "Treat your application as a journal submission" – have made you think a little differently about promotion applications.

In the next three chapters, I will demonstrate how to create a well-argued case for three core aspects of an academic job. We'll start with Research & Engagement. Teaching & Learning, and Leadership & Service will follow in the next two chapters. But first, let's discuss why evidencing your impact is so important.

Evidence helps to discount the "what ifs"

An effective promotion application is not simply a listing of your publications, the courses you have taught, and the leadership and service roles you have fulfilled. That's the stuff of your CV. To apply for promotion, you'll need a comprehensive CV. Absolutely! But a CV can only tell your promotion panel so much...

Yes, you may have top journal publications. But what if these articles were methodologically sound, but trivial in terms of their novelty or impact? What if nobody ever read or cited these articles? What if these top publications were achieved only once or twice, early in your career with the help of your PhD supervisors, never to be repeated?

A promotion panel can't discount these "what ifs" if all they have access to is your CV and a dry summary of your duties and publications. To argue a case for promotion, show your positive *impact* providing concrete *evidence*. Everyone can *claim* that they do high-quality research, are an inspirational teacher, and transformational as leaders. But how do you evidence this?

In the next three chapters, I will give you concrete examples of how to do this for Research & Engagement, Teaching & Learning, and Leadership & Service. These examples illustrate what I think is "best practice" in promotion applications. Don't worry if they seem a bit intimidating. You don't have to use them all in your own promotion application. See them as a "menu of choices" to inspire you to reflect on your own contributions. Just use whatever works best for your academic record and your institutional requirements.

Evidencing impact in Research & Engagement: the basics

Evidencing impact in this area might seem relatively easy. After all, "money talks" for successful funding applications. Publications in top journals are easily recognised in most disciplines, though it can't hurt to remind readers of these journals' standing in the field. And to evidence academic impact, you can point to citations.

All you may need to do is to contextualise your performance for the promotion panel by providing some disciplinary background and benchmarks. Below I have copied a few sections from my own promotion application to full Professor at the University of Melbourne that did exactly that.

Funding: how much is a lot?

Funding levels can differ by an order of magnitude across fields (see my blogpost "*Finding a Unicorn? Research funding in Business & Management research*"). As I knew that my promotion application would be evaluated by academics with very different expectations, it was crucial to contextualise my performance in this area. So, in my application I clarified that a $185,000 grant was exceptional in my field of Management, rather than just modest to middling as it might appear from a Life Sciences perspective.

In Melbourne, I have taken every available opportunity to apply for research funding. I have secured a University Early Career Grant (2001) of $22,000 (one of only four proposals out of fourteen that was funded), and two competitive Faculty Research grants (2002 & 2004) of $10,000 and $8,000. In 2004 I was also awarded $185,000 in ARC Discovery Grant funding for a 3-year research project, where I am the only Chief Investigator. This project deals with the impact of language on management practices within MNCs (for more detail see future research plans in Part C). This was the largest ARC discovery grant awarded to a sole Chief Investigator for a project in the subject area of Management since 2002 (no data available before that time). I received 98% of the funding I requested, which is unique as the normal average funding level lies around 70% and for management projects is usually even lower. I also received funding for a 50% relief of duties, which is hardly ever awarded.

What are top journals anyway?

In many institutions you are expected to show that you have published at least *some* of your work in journals that are among the best in the field. So, what's the problem? Surely everyone knows what these top journals are. Yes, nearly every professor in your own field will instantly recognise top journals by their titles. However, this is not the case for outsiders, even if they are in a neighbouring field.

Hence in justifying the quality of journal outlets academics will often refer to journal rankings. For some examples of these rankings, see the Journal Quality List that I have maintained since 2000, available from Harzing.com. Your university may have a list of "preferred journals". If not, use either one of the JQL rankings or a citation-based journal metric such as Clarivate's Journal Impact Factor or Elsevier's CiteScore. Make sure you contextualise these citation metrics by field. Here is how I did this in my 2006 promotion application.

Evaluating journal quality is fraught with problems. However, there can be little argument that the journals I have published in are among the top-ranked journals in Management. I will use SSCI impact scores to illustrate this. Impact scores in Management are much lower than in the Sciences or even in Management's foundation disciplines of Economics, Sociology and Psychology. An impact score of > 1.0 is generally considered to be reflective of an absolute top-level journal, while an impact score between 0.5 and 1.0 is reflective of a very good international journal. Only 30 journals in Management have impact scores above 1.0 and only 56 have an impact score above 0.5.

Note that the JIFs in this example might appear to be very low by today's standards. That is because – with publications expanding at 10% per year – average citation levels have increased dramatically in the last 15 years. In 2021, the Journal Impact Factor of the top journals in Management is well over 5. However, the general principle of comparisons is still valid.

Note also that judging publications by the ranking of the journal in which they were published is a practice that has been discredited by the Declaration on Research Assessment (DORA). More and more universities have signed this declaration. Personally, I am not a fan of journal rankings either. Over the years, I have written a lot about this (see my blogpost *"To rank or not to rank"*), including some very critical pieces.

However, in reality many universities are still using them and, when combined with other indications of the impact of the *specific* publication – such as normalised citation rates, influential citations and / or academic impact as considered in the section below – the quality of the journal offers additional supporting evidence that may help to neutralise academics' critical natures.

Benchmarks for citation performance

Just like funding levels, citation levels vary with an order of magnitude between disciplines; they even show a strong variance between sub-disciplines. Moreover, senior academics such as Deans or Heads of Department may have been promoted at a time when citations weren't really "on the radar". Hence, they might have very little idea how to evaluate your citation records. (See also my blogpost *"Citation analysis: Tips for Deans and other administrators"*). This means you may need to provide some benchmarks in your application.

In my first (unsuccessful) application to full Professor, my citation performance was described by my Head of Department as "developing", which didn't exactly work in my favour. Yes, that's meant to be an understatement! My promotion application didn't even get past the first hurdle, the Faculty committee. Always "educate" your HoD before they write your letter of support and ask to see it to correct any factual errors. They might well refuse, but you can always ask.

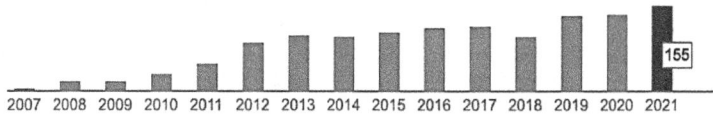

Publish or Perish

Authors	Anne-Wil Harzing
Publication date	2007
Journal	http://www.harzing.com/pop.htm
Total citations	Cited by 1290

So, in my second application, I went in "with all guns blazing" to demonstrate that my citation performance was so much more than "developing". With the help of a software programme developed with Tarma Software Research – with the ironic, tongue-in-cheek name Publish or Perish – I created a bibliometric comparison table. It showed my metrics outranked all professors in my field in Australia, all recently promoted professors in the Faculty, and many of the long-established professors. Ironically, the software programme itself is now my most-cited work (see above image).

Table 1: Bibliometric comparison with other professors, mean and range are given for each indicator.

Group	h-index	1ˢᵗ authored papers in h-index	Single-authored papers in h-index	Number of ISI citing articles (2006 only)	Number of years as professor
2005/2006 promotions	Mean: 6.3 Range: 4-8	Mean: 4.3 Range: 3-5	Mean: 3.0 Range: 2-4	Mean: 15 Range: 3-34	Recently appointed
IB professors at top Oz unis	Mean: 9.0 Range: 4-16	Mean: 3.3 Range: 1-6	Mean: 1.5 Range: 0-3	Mean: 10 Range: 3-21	15 years (4-28 years)
DoMM established professors	Mean: 14.0 Range: 6-22	Mean: 5.0 Range: 0-11	Mean: 2.0 Range: 0-4	Mean: 46 Range: 8-102	14 years (10-19 years)
Anne-Wil Harzing	13	13	10	63	N/A

Note that the h-indices and citation levels in this table – dating from 2006 – might appear to be rather low by today's standards. That is because – with publications expanding at more than 10% per year – average citation levels have increased dramatically in the last 15 years. However, the general principle of comparing your record with other professors in your institution and your general disciplines is still valid.

Depending on the level of familiarity that you expect from promotion panel to have with citation metrics, you may also need to provide a bit more background about citation analysis, data sources and the various metrics. This is how I introduced the above comparison table in my application.

> In order to put my research impact into perspective I have provided a comparison below with three groups of scholars: academics who have been promoted to professor in our Faculty in 2005/2006 (4 academics), established IB professors at UQ, Sydney and AGSM (4 academics), academics who are or recently were established professors in the Department of Management and Marketing (5 academics). Comparison is based on a number of accepted bibliometric indicators, including the recently introduced h-index[5] that has become a widely accepted "summary statistic" that combines both quantity and quality. The h index is seen to have the advantage that it gives a robust estimate of the broad impact of a scientist's cumulative research contributions. This means that the h index is insensitive to a set of lowly cited (non cited) papers or to one or several highly cited papers: A scientist with very few highly cited papers (a 'one-hit wonder') or, alternatively, many lowly cited papers will have a weak h index, whilst scientists with a steady stream of well-cited papers will have a strong h-index. The h-index was calculated using Google Scholar data. As explained earlier Google Scholar data are more comprehensive than ISI data. For comparative purposes the number of *articles* citing the academic's work in ISI journals in 2006 is also listed as a measure of contemporary influence. Please note that this figure is different from the number of *citations* as one article can (and in my cases usually does) contain multiple citations to an academic's work.

Beyond funding, top publications, and citation impact

For some universities, providing – contextualised – metrics of your research performance is all that is expected. However, for promotion to more senior positions, most universities also expect you to argue for "leadership in the academic discipline".

To establish this, it is not enough to simply rattle off in your application that you have published "five A* articles and ten A articles". You need to show *how* your research has made a real difference, ideally *both* academically and societally. Surprisingly, some academics find that really difficult to do. So, below I will provide some examples of how you can evidence both academic impact and societal impact.

Academic impact

How has your research changed the way that other academics in the field think about phenomena of interest? Has it either developed or substantially revised theories? Has it contributed new knowledge about previously under-researched phenomena or settings? Has it led the field to embark on new streams of research? Has it successfully disputed earlier findings?

You can – and obviously should – claim all of this in the description of your research programme(s). Sometimes this is enough. But without evidence "from the field" it may remain a bit of an empty claim. So, if you can draw on testimonials from other academics that will certainly help your case. But where do you get these?

Use emails and journal reviews

This is where your "good stuff file" comes in. If you dump every bit of good news into it, you don't need to waste days combing through your archives. Getting a lovely email from someone complimenting you on your paper? Take a screenshot and save it in your good stuff file. A reviewer saying something nice about your paper for a change? Make sure you record it for posterity in your good stuff file.

A few of my early publications (see blogposts "Are referencing errors undermining our scholarship and credibility?", "What if fully agree doesn't mean the same thing across cultures?", "Should we distance ourselves from the cultural distance concept?") were highly critical of earlier work in the field of International Business. Hence, it was important to show that academics in my field appreciated them.

Fortunately, I had archived an email from Michael Bond, a very prominent researcher in Cross Cultural Psychology, who – based on the first two articles – called me *"the conscience of cross-cultural psychology that keeps us all honest"*. For another article, I decided to use two journal review excerpts in my promotion application to illustrate the academic impact of my work.

This is an excellent, carefully crafted, provocative, and timely paper. I think you intelligently address an issue that should be of concern to us all.

I would like to compliment you on a very well-done paper addressing a very important issue. You have provided sound, logical, and well-established arguments as to why the field should abandon the use of a construct that has become very popular and is also used without question.

Awards signal ground-breaking contributions

Obviously, it is even better if some of your publications have won major awards. In that case you can use the laudation as independent evidence. Most of my best-paper awards came after my promotion to full professor. However, I was fortunate enough to receive one in 2005 with a very nice laudation.

This is an OS style scientific paper at its best. [...] Harzing & Sorge's findings about MNEs could be a lesson for science and for what EGOS aims at [...]; to give the floor to a diversity of expressions so that they can dialogue and cross-fertilize. To avoid normal science syndromes, let us be multinational while keeping our research fertilized by our respective "countries of origin" perspectives and traditions.

Another good way to evidence impact is to show that your articles have been reprinted in article collections. Again, I was not able to show this in my promotion application, but in the two years after my promotion to Full Professor four of my articles were reprinted in the SAGE Library series and the Routledge Critical Perspectives collections. You might be luckier and may be able to cite examples in your application.

Re-use references

Finally, when you are applying for Full Professor, you might be able to draw on a particularly evocative recommendation from your one of your referees for earlier promotion applications. Here is one from my promotion application for Associate Professor. Note how useful the last sentence is in allaying the fears discussed in Chapter 1 in the section "Understand why university promote academics".

> *In choosing her research questions, she challenges taken-for-granted assumptions, and this makes her work particularly interesting and insightful. What is also particularly commendable in her work is that she engages in difficult primary data collection, often engaging teams of collaborators, instead of following the much easier, but less insightful path of using standard published datasets and "researching under the streetlight". Her international reputation as a scholar and her ability to continue to publish intriguing articles that challenge conventional wisdom are not in doubt.*

Societal impact

Second, has your research made a difference for society? In many countries, universities are now valuing societal impact as much as academic impact. Although we cannot expect every piece of research to have direct societal impact, being able to evidence this will benefit your promotion application.

Societal impact wasn't "on the agenda" when I applied for promotion to Associate/Full Professor 15-20 years ago. So, I have provided an example from a recent application to Associate Professor by one of my colleagues Andrea Werner. She outlines the external impact of her work on the Living Wage in small and medium-sized enterprises (SMEs). See how she neatly combines her past achievements with an evidenced claim for future potential.

The LW in SMEs project forms the basis of a high-quality impact case study for the Business School's REF2021 submission, thereby evidencing the impact of my research on campaign organisations, businesses, and policy makers. Firm plans are in place to continue with LW research with a cross-disciplinary project focusing on the LW in Adult Social Care developed under my leadership.

Additional evidence of how my Middlesex University Business School colleagues have evidenced their societal impact can be seen in the video "Academics as Change Makers", a recording of a session run by the Business Ethics, CSR, and Governance Research Cluster shows. It features areas as diverse as the Living Wage, labour rights reporting and accountability and social justice in global value chains, sustainability in procurement professionals, and sexual and reproductive health of women migrant workers. You can find it on my YouTube channel "Harzing Academic Resources".

Your research standing

Beyond reporting contextualised funding, publication, and citation data, and evidencing both academic and societal impact, there are lots of other ways you can showcase your standing as a researcher, especially when applying for Associate or Full Professor. Think about editorial board memberships or editorships, evaluation of funding proposals for research councils, invitations for keynote speeches or visiting professorships.

If you play a major role in research supervision or research mentoring more generally, you are in luck! There is often some flexibility in where you can report these contributions. Research supervision and your ability to attract research students could be seen as evidence of your research prowess, but it could equally "beef up" a section on teaching & learning. Depending on its focus, research mentoring could credibly be mentioned in any of these three areas: research, teaching, and service or leadership.

At Middlesex University, long after my promotion to full professor, I embarked on a more formal role in research mentoring and staff development. However, research mentoring has been a core part of my academic identity even when I was fairly junior. So, I have drawn upon this quite heavily in my various promotion applications. It is an area in which testimonials work particularly well. Here is a lovely one from Thomas Hippler, written in the acknowledgments of his PhD. Rest in peace Thomas (see also my blogpost "*A tribute to Thomas Hippler (1972-2018)*").

> *Finally, I want to thank Dr. Anne-Wil Harzing for her encouragement and leading by example. One cannot hope for better guidance in terms of good scholarship, professional assertiveness, and personal humbleness.*

Any "extras" with that?

In justifying your impact in research & engagement, you can also bring up unique aspects of your academic record that you are proud of. In my own applications, I drew attention to the fact that my early publications in top-ranked journals were nearly all single-authored.

A remarkable aspect of my early publications in top ISI-ranked journals is that - with one exception - all nine papers are single-authored, the final paper (in *Org. Studies*) being first-authored. The four recent (2004 and 2007/2008) papers in IJHRM/HRM were co-authored. While publishing single-authored articles in these journals is relatively rare to start with (e.g., only 1 in 4 articles published in JIBS since 2000 is single-authored; for Strategic Management Journal this is only 1 in 5), publishing sole authored articles in these top journals from outside North America is very unusual. For example, I am one of only two academics associated with an Australian university who has ever published a single-authored article in *Journal of International Business Studies* (JIBS) since it was established 37 years ago. The fact that I have managed to publish a single-authored article in top (US) Management journals not just once, but no less than eight times is a unique achievement.

Another aspect of my research profile that I wanted to bring under the promotion panel's attention was my significant leadership of large-scale research projects. It was a very useful complement to my single-authored publications.

C. SIGNIFICANT ROLE IN RESEARCH PROJECTS AND INTERNATIONAL REPUTATION

Although I conduct the core of my research work individually, I have also assumed major responsibilities in research supervision and mentoring (see sub-section D), and have recently **initiated, designed and led** three large-scale international research projects. The first project dealt with the interaction between language and culture (see program 3), and involved over 30 research collaborators in 26 countries. I created the research design for the project, constructed the questionnaire with its supporting materials, and supervised the translation process for all (more than twenty) languages involved. I also recruited and managed the research collaborators through a 2-year process of data collection and consolidation. Because several collaborators in this project were PhD students or junior academics, I also fulfilled a mentoring role for many of them.

While these examples might not be applicable to you, the list of things you can use as evidence of research impact is endless. Be creative and highlight those aspects of your research career that make your application come to life. We all have diamonds in the rough in our CVs, make sure you polish them and let them shine. Next, let's turn to the two other core areas of an academic job: Teaching & Learning and Leadership & Service in the next two chapters.

Chapter 4: Evidence your impact in Teaching & Learning

Hopefully the first chapters – "Understand the process" and "Treat your application as a journal submission" – have made you think a bit differently about promotion applications.

In Chapters (3)-(5) I demonstrate how to create a well-argued case for the three core aspects of an academic job. In Chapter 3, we have started with Research & Engagement. Here we will discuss Teaching & Learning, with Leadership & Service to follow in Chapter 5. But first why is evidencing your impact so important?

Evidence helps to discount the "what ifs"

An effective promotion application is not simply a listing of your publications, the courses you have taught, and the leadership and service roles you have fulfilled. That's the stuff of your CV. To apply for promotion, you'll need a comprehensive CV. Absolutely! But a CV can only tell your promotion panel so much...

Yes, you may well have taught many courses. But what if you sent students running for cover to other electives? What if you recycled teaching materials year after year? What if your lectures induced "death by PowerPoint"? Maybe you cared mostly about teaching and "showing off" your own knowledge, and not enough about actually facilitating student learning?

A promotion panel can't discount these "what ifs" if all they have access to is your CV and a dry summary of your duties. To argue your case, you need to show your positive *impact* providing concrete *evidence*. Everyone can *claim* that they do high-quality research, are inspirational teachers, and transformational as leaders. But how do you evidence this? Below I will give you some concrete examples for Teaching & Learning.

These examples illustrate what I think is "best practice" in promotion applications. Don't worry if they seem a bit intimidating. You don't have to use them all in your own promotion application. Simply use them as a "menu of choices" to inspire you to reflect on your own contributions. Use whatever works for your academic record and your institutional requirements.

Evidencing impact in Teaching & Learning: The basics

Scope of your teaching

I know I said that you shouldn't *just* list the courses you taught. That's true, but you should list them. I suggest though that you create a concise table that doesn't just list the courses, but also the level and program, the number of students in each course, what your role was, and how much course development was involved. That way you can provide a clear overview of the significance of your contribution to teaching without taking up too much space in your application. Here is what I used in my own application.

Table 2 lists the subjects I have taught since joining the University of Melbourne. Although only *Managing Across Borders* and the two PhD subjects were completely new, I also had to redevelop most of the other subjects, because the existing teaching materials were either unavailable or outdated. Furthermore, as I only repeated one of the four subjects from my first year (mid 2001-mid 2002) at Melbourne in subsequent years, my contribution to teaching and subject development has been substantial.

Table 2: Summary of subjects taught since joining the University of Melbourne

Year	Subject	Level	# students	Role	Newly developed?	Research area?
2001	International Business Strategy (S2)	MIB	45	½ coord., ½ lectures	Yes	Partly
2001	Global Management Issues (S2)	MIB	28	½ coord., ½ lectures	Partly	Partly
2001	Strategic Management of Org. (S2)	GradDip	40	Full coord., all lectures	Yes	No
2002	Strategy (S1)	UG	320	Full coord., ½ lectures	Yes	No
2002	Global Management Issues (S2)	MIB	29	Full coord., ¾ lectures	Partly	Partly
2002	Managing Across Borders (S2)	MIB	74	Full coord., all lectures	Yes	Yes
2003	Global Management Issues (S1)	MIB	35	Full coord., all lectures	Partly	Partly
2003	Global Management Issues (S2)	MIB	35–40	Full coord., all lectures	Partly	Partly
2003	Managing Across Borders (S2)	MIB	70-80	Full coord., all lectures	Yes	Yes
2004	Global Management Issues (S1)	MIB	41	Full coord., all lectures	Partly	Partly
2005/6	Research Decisions (S1)	PhD	10 (25)*	Full coord., some lectures	Yes	Yes
2005/6	Research Methods (S1+S2)	PhD	11 (25)*	Full coord., some lectures	Yes	Yes

* Although only 10/11 first year students were registered for these subjects, many older year students attended and hence attendance in the sessions varied from 15 to 30

The table allowed me to evidence that I had taught across four levels (Graduate Diploma, Undergraduate, Postgraduate and PhD) and that I had experience in both smaller and larger classes.

Most importantly though it allowed me to evidence that I had taken on a major coordinating role in all these courses and that all of them involved at least some course development. It also evidenced that I had been prepared to teach courses outside of my area of research.

Your teaching evaluations

Many universities have quantitative student evaluations. There is significant controversy over the extent to which such measures accurately reflect teaching proficiency. However, if your evaluations are fine, by all means give them a prominent place in your application.

My teaching evaluations are good and at or above the Departmental and Faculty average. For the UG subject Strategy I spent a lot of time redesigning the subject completely, producing a very extensive course outline and a 50-page tutorial manual. I also introduced the use of Webraft as a teaching support mechanism. This was very successful and was highly used with an average of 2,500 server requests a week. Comments about my share of the lecturing on the QoT forms for Strategy were highly positive.

Table 3: Summary of teaching evaluations at the University of Melbourne 2001-2004 (scale 1-5)

Question	Global Mgt Issues (01-04) MIB	Managing Across Borders (02-03) MIB	International Business Strategy MIB	Strategic Mgmt of Org. (Grad Dip)	Strategy UG*
I had a clear idea what was expected of me	4.1	3.9	4.0	3.8	3.6
This subject was well taught	4.1	4.2	4.0	3.8	3.6
This subject was intellectually stimulating	3.8	4.0	3.9	3.8	3.5
I received helpful feedback on how I was going	4.1	3.8	3.6	3.8	2.6
Interest in the academic needs of the students	4.2	4.1	4.0	4.0	3.4

* The quantitative teaching evaluations for Strategy were not differentiated by lecturer (I took only half of the lectures), nor were tutors evaluated separately. Hence the QoT scores do not necessarily reflect the quality of my own teaching.

My QoT results for postgraduate teaching are generally good and for the Master's in international business compare favourably with the average teaching scores for this degree. These evaluations are particularly pleasing since I insist on academically rigorous work and am not a lenient marker. Two typical quotes from QoT forms are included. Other quotes are available upon request.

The most interesting subject in the MIB for me. Anne-Wil showed great knowledge in this field and transferred it to us in an entertaining way. I also enjoyed the unusual assignment of the culture visit. I learned a lot!

Anne-Wil is very well organised, clear, articulate and clearly an expert in her field. This subject has fitted well with others in the MIB program and helped non-Australian students integrate with each other and local students. Classes are participative and good range of teaching styles/materials are used.

Again, I suggest you create a concise table (see above) that packs in a lot of information. You can also add a few explanatory notes and throw in a few nice student comments. As you can see my teaching evaluations were good (above the Dept and Faculty average), but not exceptional. So, beyond "explaining away" the low score for one subject, which was co-taught with a colleague whose lectures were very poorly received, I didn't dwell on my teaching performance.

Turn a negative into a positive

If your quantitative teaching evaluations haven't been universally high, you can use your promotion application to contextualise these. Doing so may turn a negative into a positive.

My own early teaching evaluations at the University of Melbourne were marred by student concerns about my high marking standards. This is how I turned this around in my promotion application.

> After early student concerns about my high marking standards, I have started to make my expectations in terms of rigorous academic work even clearer at the start of semester and provide standard feedback sheets, on which students are marked on ten specific criteria and receive extensive additional written suggestions for improvement. The response to this initiative has been extremely positive. Many students have substantially improved their essay writing skills and now receive much higher marks, even though my marking standards are unchanged. Focused feedback seems to have created a strong desire to do well for my subjects, illustrated by comments such as: *"I'll try to do better in the next assignment. I won't let you down!"* and *"I am so encouraged by my high mark, since I know you have very high standards."*

Having "negatives" in your promotion application isn't as bad as you might think it is. In a way it increases the credibility of your application as none of us are without flaws. It also makes you appear more human, which is never a bad thing ☺.

Most importantly, it gives you an opportunity to show that you *learn* from your mistakes and that you are willing to invest time and effort into improving your performance. This is important as it allays the promotion committee's fear that you "might rest on your laurels" when getting promoted.

Your university might also use peer evaluations of your teaching. These can be a goldmine of evidence in your promotion applications as they generally offer a much more rounded perspective of teaching quality than relying on students alone. Your colleagues are likely to take a much broader perspective of teaching and learning than your students.

However, most of your efforts in the teaching and learning space happen outside formal classroom sessions. So, by necessity this means that formal teaching evaluations only capture a small part of what we do as university lecturers. So, what else can you use to build your case on teaching?

Teaching philosophy

First, you can make your teaching case more forceful by framing it within a clearly articulated teaching philosophy. To be frank, I wouldn't label my own – fairly weak – attempt below as such, but it did provide a general statement of the principles underlying my teaching. This statement will already tell your evaluation panel that you approach your teaching reflectively.

> Because of the multi-faceted and integrative nature of the subjects that I teach, all of my current modules have been designated as coursework-only modules. The coursework is not of the one-size-fits-all type, but is explicitly aimed at letting students develop their own capabilities. My teaching is supported by up-to-date technological aids, including PowerPoint slides, videos, and traditional and computer-based simulations. My newly developed subject for the Masters in International Business (*Managing Across Borders*) includes an even wider range of teaching methods, and includes a guided "culture visit" that allows students to apply their theoretical knowledge in practice. Many students have told me that they dreaded this assignment, but have learned an enormous amount from it.

You might be quite amused by seeing PowerPoint slides and videos described as up-to-date technological aids. Remember though this was written nearly twenty years ago! The general principle would still applies though, show your panel that you are familiar with all the latest techniques in supporting good teaching practices. Since the COVID19 pandemic this obviously includes being an effective and inclusive online teacher.

Course development and research-based teaching

You might also be expected to show how you bring research into the classroom to ensure your students have access to recent research and help them develop their critical thinking skills. Providing concrete examples of how you have done this in practice is very helpful. Here is a very effective attempt at this by my Middlesex colleague Andrea Werner in her application for promotion to Associate Professor.

> *My research-led (re-)design of ethics modules is underpinned by our cross-departmental research cluster Business Ethics, CSR, and Governance (which I am co-leading) ensuring a strong research-teaching nexus. Our cluster's institutional partnership with the Institute of Business Ethics ensures that their resources support the development of high-quality courses that create career opportunities for our students.*

My Middlesex colleague Satkeen Azizzadeh's research interests in the same field were also very effectively incorporated in her successful application for promotion to Senior Lecturer. Here she describes the redesign of the core/compulsory module Management Concepts, which is offered across the largest undergraduate programme in the University. She not only consulted widely with internal stakeholders, but also analysed what other universities were delivering and spoke to her network of contacts in the public and private sector for input on potential topics, skills, and competencies that they would consider appropriate for hiring graduates in contemporary organisations.

> *As a result of this extensive process of consultation, I incorporated a range of core topics, […] vital for success in the workplace. To enhance students' understanding of the theoretical concepts and their application within the workplace, I chose relevant case studies and exercises in the seminars. Furthermore, I have incorporated my own research on CSR and Knowledge Management in the curriculum.*

Creating an inclusive classroom

Many universities, and especially those in Anglophone countries, now have many international students. At Middlesex University we have 150 different nationalities represented on our three campuses in London, Mauritius, and Dubai. Hence the ability to create an inclusive classroom is a very important teaching skill in most universities. Here is an example of how one of my Middlesex colleagues, Satkeen Azizzadeh, evidenced this in her (successful) application to Senior Lecturer.

> *I am aware and respectful of the diverse range of our students' cultural and educational backgrounds. [...] For example, when students have a question or make an observation, my reply is to affirm them through positive constructive formative feedback. [...] If a student is anxious or I feel they are concerned about how their question could be perceived by others, I emphasise what an excellent question this is and that their peers might be interested to note down my response in view of my answer possibly being of use in their assessments. I believe this practice to be very valuable in building confidence in students, particularly those who are from cultures where individualism is not the norm.*

Of course, it is even more powerful if you can also evidence that this practice works and that it leads to positive student outcomes. Satkeen was able to do so very effectively.

> *During the past few years, some of my students who began the term by being hesitant to contribute in seminars have gained confidence and enhanced their performance. Many of these students achieved a First overall for the Module and participation became a norm for them by the end of the Module. I received outstanding feedback and thank you notes from these students stating that I was an exceptional teacher in terms of empowering them to believe in themselves and to be successful.*

Designing assessment and feedback

Many universities will expect you to show how you design assessment and feedback to facilitate learning. Here is a great example by my Middlesex University colleague Andrea Werner. Note how she neatly wraps in diversity in the classroom too.

> In [...] assessment and feedback, I emphasise application of conceptual knowledge to real life cases to equip students with important analytical skills. For UG assignments I create case vignettes based on current business ethics news. At PG level, students choose an ethics news story, an ethical issue affecting their organisation, or a personal ethical workplace dilemma for analysis. This enables co-curricular experience where students co-create knowledge and insight into ethical issues in the workplace and are able to draw on their diverse backgrounds in their learning and development.

Satkeen Azizzadeh's statement is also very effective in combining a general statement about the role of assessment in her modules with examples.

> Assessments for all of my modules are designed to enhance a deeper comprehension of the key concepts covered during taught sessions. Assessments are also designed to develop students' skills and competencies that enhance their employability. For instance, students are required to produce a professionally structured business report which enables them to analyse and apply their theoretical knowledge to a real-life organisation such as Tesla or Amazon.

Teaching & learning:
much more than classroom activities

In 2022 Middlesex University completely revamped its promotion guidelines. In doing so it included no less than eight aspects of teaching and learning. Regardless of the institution you work for, you might find them helpful to broaden the scope of your teaching case.

1. Academic and pastoral support for learners – making learner wellbeing core to all we do by providing support which encourages engagement with learning, generating pride and a sense of belonging

2. Equality, Diversity, and Inclusion – actions that ensure teaching speaks to our learners' experiences and reduces differences in outcomes related to backgrounds or prior attainment

3. Support for learning – design of learning, assessment and feedback which allows students to develop as confident and independent learners, allowing learners to seek out new experiences, explore new perspectives and achieve their goals

4. Teaching – demonstrating the university's commitment to co-creation, active and practice-based learning, and reflected in and evidenced by a record of excellent teaching / module evaluations

5. Curriculum Development – development of new or redesigned modules, courses or training materials that address societal concerns, explore new perspectives, and/or create career opportunities for students

6. Approaches to learning – staying abreast of good practice and using evidence, innovation, and research to continually enhance teaching and learning and bring student success

7. Leadership of educational activity within the University – investing in supporting the development of ECAs, and / or development of pedagogic projects and policies that demonstrate positive impact on the student experience or outcomes

8. Peer esteem - invited roles in external initiatives, awards etc.

Leadership in teaching

A good overview of the different types of teaching performance expected at different levels can be found in *The Career Framework for University Teaching* by Ruth Graham. This is particularly useful for those who aim for academic career progression predominantly based on their contribution to teaching and learning.

For more senior positions, it might also help to evidence that your research is used by other lecturers. Likewise, especially if you work at a teaching-intensive university, you might want to show that you have developed teaching materials that are used outside your own institution.

An excellent way to do this is using Open Syllabus (See my blogpost *"Open Syllabus Explorer: evidencing research-based teaching?"*). This is particularly helpful if you have authored a textbook; obviously textbooks are more likely to appear in syllabi than academic articles.

For instance, using Open Syllabus I was able to show that my IHRM textbook appeared more than 500 time in syllabi. I discovered it was used not just in universities in the UK, North America, and Australia, but also in a variety of European countries and in more than three dozen Indian universities. How cool is that?

Don't give up on your academic articles though. You might well be pleasantly surprised! 36 of my academic articles appeared in syllabi. If you are junior, you are unlikely to have many articles featured in syllabi, but even if you find only one case that can still be argued to be indicative of future leadership in teaching.

In sum

Having discussed Research & Engagement and Teaching & Learning in Chapters 3 and 4, we will focus on Leadership & Service in Chapter 5. Note that in Chapter 5 we will focus on specific leadership roles. However, as you have seen in this chapter, as well as Chapter 3 where we discussed Research & Engagement, for more senior positions universities will often expect you to display leadership in *every* area of your academic job.

Chapter 5: Evidence your impact in Leadership & Service

Hopefully the first two chapters – "Understand the process" and "Treat your application as a journal submission" – have made you think a little differently about promotion applications.

In Chapters (3)-(5) I demonstrate how to create a well-argued case for the three core aspects of an academic job. In previous chapters we discussed Research & Engagement and Teaching & Learning. In this chapter we will focus on Leadership & Service. But first, why is evidencing your impact so important?

Evidence helps to discount the "what ifs"

An effective promotion application is not simply a listing of your publications, the courses you have taught, and the leadership and service roles you have fulfilled. That's the stuff of your CV. To apply for promotion, you'll need a comprehensive CV. Absolutely! But a CV can only tell your promotion panel so much...

Yes, you may have been Head of Department. But what if more than half of the Department's staff members left during your tenure? Yes, you may have been the department's seminar coordinator. But what if most seminars started late, were chaotic, and attendance dropped. Yes, you may have been a member of many committees. But what if all you did was sit through the meetings in silence?

A promotion panel can't discount these "what ifs" if they only have access to your CV and a dry summary of your duties and output. To argue your case, you need to show your positive impact providing concrete evidence. Everyone can *claim* they do high-quality research, are inspirational teachers, and transformational as leaders. But how do you evidence this? Below I will give you some concrete examples for Leadership & Service.

These examples illustrate what I think is "best practice" in promotion applications. Don't worry if they seem a bit intimidating. You don't have to use them all in your own promotion application. Just see them as a "menu of choices" to inspire you to reflect on your own contributions. Use whatever works for your academic record and your institutional requirements.

Evidencing impact in Leadership & Service:
On job titles and beyond...

Both research & engagement and teaching & learning have generally accepted "objective" performance indicators such as publications, funding, citations, and teaching evaluations. These indicators may well be flawed, but they *are* commonly used and well accepted in promotion applications.

Making a case for the positive impact of your leadership and service to the university (or wider academic profession) might be a bit harder as there are no clear-cut indicators. So, you need to a bit more creative to evidence your contributions in this area.

What is most important is to keep in mind that leadership and service is not simply a matter of job roles and titles. Yes, having taken on these positions is better than not having done any of them. But it is entirely possible for bad or just mediocre performance in leadership and service to go unnoticed. Unlike research and teaching, there are usually few established accountability mechanisms for leadership and service in universities.

So, your promotion panel will want to know what lies *behind* that job title. They want to know whether your involvement in a particular leadership or service activity has *made a difference*. Especially when you apply for promotion to Associate Professor or Full Professor, it is not enough to simply "sit on a committee" or "take your turn" as programme leader or seminar organizer.

It is all about how *your* presence has changed the university or the academic community for the better. So, let's look at how this would work in practice. Below, I provide three suggestions: point to specific initiatives and qualitative change, show positive changes in hard metrics, and use testimonials from students and colleagues.

Point to specific initiatives and qualitative change

First, make sure that you provide a synopsis of what the leadership or service role involves. Remember, this might not be common knowledge. Moreover, these functions might include very different responsibilities across universities, or even Faculties, Schools, and Departments.

Second, point to *specific* initiatives that you have developed during your tenure. This shows that you didn't just take on a "caretaker" role, but tried actively to improve outcomes. Here is mine for my role as Director of the PhD program at the University of Melbourne. Note that I didn't only list the initiatives, but also tried to evidence their positive impact in general qualitative terms. You might be able to write up something similar in your own application for other types of programme director roles.

Currently, my most significant administrative task in the department is the directorship of the PhD program. At the moment we have about 75 students enrolled in our PhD program. I am responsible for selection of candidates and am Chair of both the Confirmation (defence of research proposal at the end of the first year) and Examination Committee. I am also coordinator of the PhD coursework modules. In my role as PhD director, I have introduced the following significant changes to improve the program:

1. I tightened up the confirmation requirements, a process that was started by the previous PhD director. I have introduced written comments on the Confirmation Report in the form of memos ranging from 2 to 5 single-spaced pages. Students are normally requested to submit a revised confirmation report before they are confirmed.
2. I provide significant academic support to students on a regular basis by circulating information on conferences, journals, academic positions, useful websites, etc.
3. I introduced two PhD coursework modules, a process that was started by the previous PhD director. These modules were first offered in 2005 and there is general agreement in the department that they have significantly improved the quality and consistency of our students' work.

If necessary, you can also provide a bit more detail about individual activities and evidence positive impact through testimonials.

In 2005, the Department of Management introduced two PhD coursework modules into the PhD program. As director of the PhD program, I was given the responsibility to coordinate both modules. As there are more than 20 academics teaching into the coursework, coordinating it is a very significant administrative task. Despite some teething problems, student feedback was generally highly positive, and the modules seem to have benefited students from all year groups. Some representative student comments in the QOT:

> *Congratulations on doing a great job and raising the standard of the PhD course. I wish I had the benefit of some courses as "refreshers" early in my PhD studies and I wouldn't be on extensions now.*

> *Thank you for an unforgettable period of stimulation, enrichment, and exposure to some incredible academic role models. These courses have been the highlight of my candidature at Melbourne University.*

Show positive changes in "hard metrics"

Although providing evidence of specific initiatives is already a big improvement over job titles, this doesn't always tell the panel whether these initiatives were successful. Above I tried to argue for positive impact, but I was unable to provide any "hard metrics". The university's systems at the time were simply not set up for this.

If your university does have good monitoring systems, you may be able to point to positive changes in quantitative terms. For teaching-related roles this could be metrics such as growing student numbers for a programme, improvements in the National Student Surveys, an increase in the proportion of students receiving scholarships, or an increase in timely completion. Although I did not have access to hard metrics like this for my PhD directorship, I was able to point to some key changes that were indisputable:

> *I led a major review of the Department's PhD programme in 2006 and have already implemented many of its recommendations. For the first time since inception of the programme, PhD students now receive substantial resources for conference attendance and fieldwork. I also ensured that all PhD students were provided with the facility to create their own home pages.*

For research-related leadership roles you could refer to increases in international research rankings or to national research evaluations, such as the REF (Research Excellence Framework) in the UK. That said, remember that the more distant these metrics are to the outcome, the less convincing they will be. This is how argued this for the impact of my role in research mentoring and staff development at Middlesex University in my performance appraisal.

Obviously, it not possible to establish conclusively a direct link between MUBS investing in a supportive and collaborative research culture and improved research outcomes. That said, it is probably no coincidence that, since 2016, Middlesex University in general – and the Business School in particular – have substantially improved their position in the four major international research rankings: the Times Higher Education ranking, the Times Higher Education Young Universities ranking, the ARWU Shanghai ranking, and the US NEWS Best Global Universities ranking.

Testimonials from students and colleagues

Anne-Wil Harzing Professor of International Management, Middlesex University December 16, 2018, Mariana worked with Anne-Wil in the same group	Mariana is simply the best Head of Department I have encountered in my journeys in academia in the last 28 years. She is able to combine strategic vision with due attention to the day-to-day minutia. Mariana is encouraging and respectful towards both academic and professional staff and readily makes time for both of them. She genuinely enjoys the job and wants to do it well, not for the glory or the power, but because she thinks it is an important job. I praise myself lucky to be working with her to realise the Middlesex University Business School's tremendous research potential. **See less**

Testimonials from other people are an excellent way to evidence your impact in the leadership and service area. Over the years I received many lovely emails from colleagues relating to my roles in research leadership at the University of Melbourne, my service to the wider academic community through the Publish or Perish software in the past fifteen years, my role in staff development and research mentoring at Middlesex University, and my work as founder of the CYGNA women's network.

However, I would never have been able to collate these examples for my promotion application and later applications for Fellowships and Awards if I had not maintained a "nice emails" folder in my mailbox. This can be a major source for your "good stuff file" (see Chapter 1).

I also write plenty of testimonials and thank-you emails myself (see also my blogpost *"Changing academic culture: one email at a time..."*). Above is one that I wrote for our wonderful Head of Department Mariana Dodourova. Consider posting testimonials on your LinkedIn profile. This makes it much easier for people to refer to them when applying for promotion.

Under the banner "2022 The Year of Positive Academia" I have started to write testimonials for colleagues, mentees, co-authors, and others I admire (see also my post "Using LinkedIn recommendations to support others"). To date I have written more than 55 and I have no intention to stop ☺. Although my testimonials were unsolicited, don't hesitate to ask people to write these for you if you think they are justified. If you do a good job, most colleagues are happy to do you a favour, they just need a little prompting.

Service to the academic community

For academic service work, you can often refer to material that is publicly available. For instance, to evidence your involvement in reviewing you might consider setting up a Publons profile.

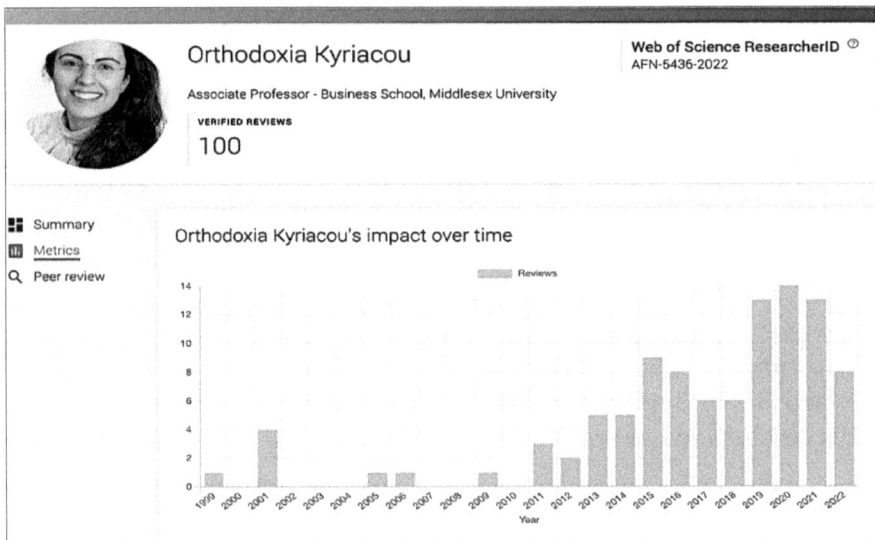

Orthodoxia Kyriacou
Associate Professor - Business School, Middlesex University

Web of Science ResearcherID ⑦
AFN-5436-2022

VERIFIED REVIEWS
100

■■ Summary
▥ Metrics
Q Peer review

Orthodoxia Kyriacou's impact over time

This allows you to "claim" reviews you have done. The image above shows the Publons account of one of my colleagues, Dox Kyriacou, who is an avid reviewer.

If, like me, you run an academic website or blog like me, page visits and ranking in global internet traffic (see below) are good metrics to evidence impact. For some of these metrics you might need to provide some context. Here's how I would do this for my website:

> *"In evaluating website rankings, it helps to know that there are currently about 1.2 billion websites, with 200 million of those active. So, my website ranks in the top 0.1% of active websites in terms web traffic."*

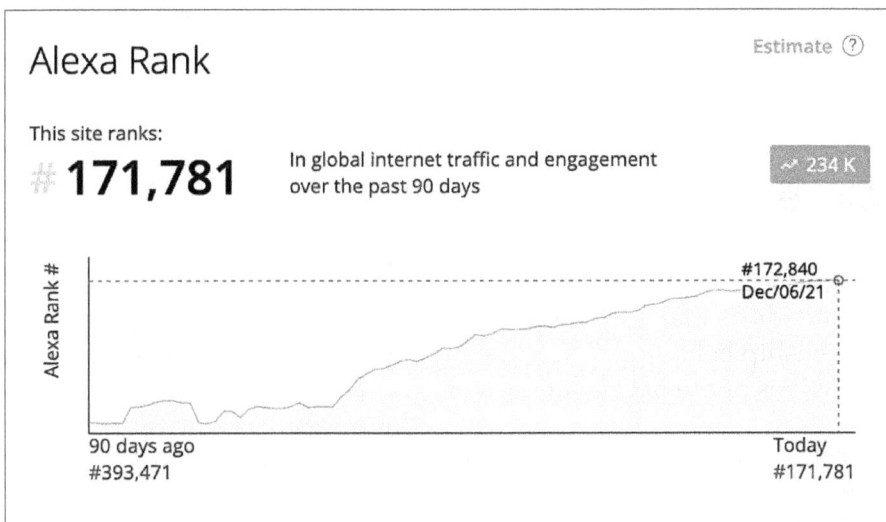

Alexa Rank

Estimate ⑦

This site ranks:

171,781

In global internet traffic and engagement over the past 90 days

↗ 234 K

Alexa Rank #

#172,840
Dec/06/21

90 days ago
#393,471

Today
#171,781

For academic service work that relates to a specific *position*, you can use the same strategy as I outlined above for leadership positions in your own institution. Here is an example of one of my early leadership roles, one that I took on just before I was appointed as Senior Lecturer.

From 2001-2003, I was Chair of the newly established Membership Involvement Committee (MIC) of the Intl. Management Division (IMD) of the Academy of Management. The MIC was established to assist the IMD Executive Council in identifying and addressing issues regarding member relations and involvement. I was invited to become Chair because of my broad international network of contacts.

Since barriers for active participation in the Academy are often higher for non-US members, I recruited nearly 50 country representatives, covering more than 40 countries, to help in the running of the MIC. These country representatives acted as a liaison between academics in their own country and myself as Chair of the MIC. To facilitate interaction with IMD members, short bios and pictures of all country reps were included on my web site. Information about activities of the MIC was distributed via the IMD mailings list and newsletter (I wrote a report for each newsletter) and via www.harzing.com.

In addition to regular communication about internationalisation issues with the IMD Executive Committee, I developed several initiatives in my role of MIC chair. First, since professional development workshops are an important way to involve members in the division, I organised a PDW on "Doing International Research" for the 2002 Academy meeting. This PDW included presenters from five different countries. Second, I organised an evening at the yearly meeting to introduce new and international members to the Academy. This evening consisted of three parts: a reception, a "roadmap to the Academy" and a "take-a-member-of the-Executive-to-dinner". This has since become a regular part of the IMD conference program.

Make invisible work visible

The problem with service work is that much of it is "invisible". This is true for formal administrative positions as well as "organisational citizenship behaviour". It is the type of work that has been identified as "wives of the organisation work".

For more detail on this see Anne Huff's wonderful article: Wives of the organisation. It is more than 30 years old, but has lost none of its potency. Here are some excerpts.

> *Almost all the female professionals I know are overly committed to time consuming but often unnoticed and unrewarded aspects of organizational life. [...] First of all, the organization wife recognizes personal differences, is usually aware of other people's needs, and tries to fill those needs. [...] Because we recognize these things more often, because we think about them more often, we are more likely to do something about them.*

"... being an administrator is the worst of being the traditional wife. What those around you want are hot meals on time. They do not want to know how it is done. They rarely say thank you. Nonetheless it all has to be done over again the next day."

So, whether you are female, male, or non-binary: if you are a "wife of the organisation", feel free to make your invisible, but invaluable work, visible by mentioning it in your promotion application. This is especially true for organisational citizenship behaviour that often isn't recognised in promotion guidelines. One note of caution here – don't go overboard, especially if you are a woman.

While warmth is seen as positive for all professionals, women are caught in an unfortunate paradox. Women considered not warm enough are likely to be described as too competitive, or even considered to be "a bitch" – and yet if considered too warm this may detract from their perceived competence (for an excellent analysis see: "What if warmth/competence for women is not a matrix but a spectrum?"). Here is my modest addition in a 20-page application.

> In addition to the formal memberships and activities, I take a strong interest in the social functioning of the department. I was the initiator and organiser of a monthly women's lunch and always attended the social gatherings for the program I was most heavily involved with (Masters in International Business). I have also been involved in the organisation of the 2002 Christmas function and organised several welcome dinners for new members of staff at my home.

My amazing Middlesex colleague Satkeen Azizzadeh would be able to write pages on this. In her successful application for promotion to Senior Lecturer she also sensibly kept it to a modest few sentences.

Fortunately, she asked me to be one of her referees and I was able to elaborate on this to do full justice to this time-consuming role. Rest assured that I only did so *after* writing in equally effusive terms about her strong abilities as a researcher.

Collegiality

Although collegiality is essential for the smooth functioning of *any* organisation, as well as the well-being of its employees, promotion guidelines in most universities emphasize individual achievements and reinforce competition. In 2022 Middlesex University completely revamped its promotion criteria. The new criteria make collegiality an explicit element of any application.

> *Collegiality is seen as a key factor in ensuring the successful implementation of the Strategy and so it is a core criterion for promotion. All candidates must explicitly demonstrate how they have upheld the principles of the University and provide evidence of how they contribute to the delivery of the University Strategy.*

The guidelines suggest that evidencing good academic citizenship can take many forms and includes:

- Contributing to an inclusive community through promoting equality and diversity.

- Supporting the career development of colleagues, including mentoring, support, peer review and relevant collaborations, particularly in relation to early career colleagues.

- Voluntary or civic engagement activities in line with the University's strategic goals.

- Taking on Departmental, Faculty or University roles which may be over and above what may be expected.

Committee membership:
how (not) to evidence this?

Most of the examples above deal with major leadership roles that might be quite rare at early career stages. However, nearly all of us have some experience with committee membership. So, how do you make the most of this in your application? The below example shows four ways in which you can write this up. It is based on my own experience as an early career member of the research committee in the late 1990s.

1. *Role-based*: "I was the ECR (i.e., early career researcher) member of the research committee." This is not very effective as it could mean anything from skipping three quarters of the meetings and sitting silent in the others, to transforming the life of ECRs in your institution.

2. *Activity-based*: "As an ECR member of the research committee, I solicited feedback actively from other junior staff so that I could represent their perspective. I also volunteered to investigate our institution's journal ranking list. This involved collating journal rankings from other institutions in the UK and abroad." This is more effective as it demonstrates both an active role, as well as concrete initiatives.

3. *Impact-based*: "I was an advocate for ECRs on the research committee and ensured improved conditions for junior staff". Whilst this might *sound* nice, without specifics and evidence it is a rather empty claim. So, whilst better than #1, it is not very effective.

4. *Evidence-based impact*: "As a result of my research into journal rankings, the School changed the journal rankings that it used for tenure and promotion decisions. This led to more equality between different sub-disciplines in the School."

A combination of 2 & 4 transforms a boring committee membership into a strong contribution. It also documented that I was willing to go the extra mile in helping the university change its systems for the better. The resulting collated list of journal rankings was also one of the first resources to be posted on my academic website, which I had created soon after.

Career narrative

The example of my role as ECR member of the research committee could have been used in later promotion applications to document my early interest in research evaluation. This interest ultimately led to the Journal Quality List (2000), now in its 69th edition, and the Publish or Perish software (2007). It was also the beginning of what is now among the 0.1% most visited websites in the world (see above).

Finally, it led to a brand-new research programme on the "Quality and Impact of Academic Research" with dozens of publications on the role of editors and editorial boards in the publishing process, the development of new citation-based metrics, the role of bibliometrics in the Social Sciences, and national research evaluations. The latest publication is a 2020 book chapter "Everything you always wanted to know about impact...."

If I had to apply for promotion today, it would have given me a very nice career narrative ☺. And this brings us to the topic of the next Chapter: Craft your career narrative.

Chapter 6: Craft your career narrative

Evidencing your positive impact for the core aspects of an academic job – Research & Engagement, Teaching & Learning, Leadership & Service – is crucial. Additionally, especially when applying for promotion to Associate or Full Professor, universities might also want to know what you "profess". In other words, a (coherent) statement of what you see as the core of your academic identity.

Drawing on your academic identity can turn your application from a fairly sterile list of achievements to a compelling career narrative. It demonstrates you are an individual who cares about their profession, rather than a cardboard cut-out rattling off a list of tick-boxes.

Finding your career narrative is not always easy. Some academics are able to craft this narrative prospectively, others construct it retrospectively – perhaps even drawing inspiration from how others see them. Below I have provided examples for each of these three options.

Craft your career narrative prospectively

For some academics a career narrative comes naturally and dates from the very start of their careers. These are often academics who have either very focused research interests or a burning passion for a particular field of research.

One of my colleagues, Andrea Werner, recently applied successfully for promotion to Associate Professor. Her application had a very clear narrative around her interest in Business Ethics and CSR. This was reflected in both her contribution to research and to teaching.

My research interest in Business Ethics and Corporate Social Responsibility derives from my belief that business should be a force for good in society. I thus have a passion for applied research that, in line with the University's aim, "has a positive impact in society".

I am passionate about teaching Business Ethics; I believe today's business world requires a thorough understanding of ethical and social responsibility issues. Through my teaching, students develop crucial employability skills such as analytical and critical thinking, developing solutions to ethical issues, and the ability to speak up about misconduct.

However, it was also evident in her leadership, which – in addition to being PhD coordinator and departmental seminar coordinator – involved appointments as a reviewer for the Departmental Research Ethics Committee (REC), editorial board member for the *Journal of Business Ethics*, a premier journal in the field, and co-lead of a research cluster in Business Ethics and Corporate Governance.

Hence, her passions and strengths were abundantly clear from her application. They also provided an excellent match with the need of the university and the school. As Andrea also effectively evidenced her performance in research, teaching, and leadership, the decision to promote her is likely to have been an easy one.

Many of my Middlesex Business School colleagues have an equally burning research passion that guides their career. Here is a selection that might inspire you to write your own:

- Anastasia Christou: My interdisciplinary research on the inequalities of gender, class, race/ethnicity, sexualities in migrant-/minority, youth/ageing groups advances decolonial contributions and transnational ethical awareness toward social justice, inclusivity, and equity.

- Parisa Dashtipour: My research explores the organisational and psychosocial dynamics that shape and limit mental health at work.

- Athina Dilmperi: My research examines how consumption can improve well-being, focusing on how lives can be enriched by the creative/cultural and recreation domains. I collaborate with industry and policy makers to provide solutions that increase societal well-being.

- Tim Freeman: My research explores issues of public service delivery, policy and governance, and my current and recent funded projects and publications have an economic development emphasis in relation to migrant communities within the UK and global south.

- Yan Jiang: My research explores how to manage and achieve sustainability in the supply chain. My research is closely related to industry, involving relationship management, mutual influence, and key performance outcomes for supply chain members.

- Nico Pizzolato: My research looks at the transformation of capitalism over the past century and the changing role and subjectivities of workers in it; within this horizon, I focus on labour migration; coercion and labour; workplace democracy.

- Ericka Rascon Ramirez: My research focuses on the causes of low investments in human capital. I use economic and social psychology theories to inform the design of interventions that aim to improve learning, sexual health, and civic education in Africa and Middle East.

- Salma Soliman: My passion for multi-disciplinary research leads me to explore different topics and industries (e.g., global value chains, refugee entrepreneurship, agro-industry, hotel industry) under the general umbrella of institutional voids in emerging markets (EMs).

- Clarice Santos: My research interests reflect my commitment to, and passion for, diversity, equality, inclusion, and, ultimately, social justice. I use community building and engagement to co-create better futures, focusing particularly on women and ethnic minorities.

Create your career narrative retrospectively

Not all of us have such a strong narrative running through our own career. I very much "stumbled into" a PhD and an academic career. I chose my research topics based on whatever fascinated me at the time or the practical challenges that I encountered, rather than having a burning research passion. So, I certainly didn't have a coherent narrative ready when I started writing my promotion application.

But sometimes you can craft this narrative retrospectively. You might be able to deduce it from a pattern of actions, much like an emergent strategy. This might not be possible for your entire career profile, but you may be able to do this for one or more elements of your promotion application.

When I crafted my promotion application for Associate Professor, I really struggled to tie together five different research programmes. However, after some reflection I was able to capture the principles underlying them (see below) and was able to write up the remainder of application evidencing these principles.

> *My approach to research has been guided by three key principles: conducting innovative research in new areas; designing rigorous, systematic, and large-scale empirical tests of core models and theories in international management; and challenging commonly held beliefs through a critical evaluation of established work. As a result, my research has consistently pushed the frontiers in International Management and has become highly cited by academics in the field.*

My teaching statement was also fairly generic. To make my case, I relied on the breadth of the courses I had taught, my good teaching evaluations, and my textbook in International HRM. At the time it wasn't yet necessary to establish you had taught according to the 7, 8, 9, 10, 11, 12, 13 or even 20 "principles of effective teaching", and/or embodied the "values of the university" through your teaching.

However, I think I did manage to find a coherent – retrospective – rationale for my approach to leadership. What do you think?

There are so many opportunities for leadership in University management that it is difficult to know where to channel one's efforts. I found that one of the best places for me to show leadership was in a place that would capitalise on my research skills and my passion for mentoring, so I've taken on a large-scale Departmental role – the directorship of the PhD program. [...] I was also able to express this through the development and maintenance of my academic website, www.harzing.com, into a major resource centre in international and cross-cultural management.

For those that are cynical about these exercises in "story-telling", I am not suggesting you disingenuously invent a story. What I am suggesting is that you use your promotion application as a reflection on what is important to you. Your evaluators will find it much easier to appreciate your contributions if they display some coherence.

Be inspired by colleagues' view of your work

You know how readers sometimes find meanings in a poem that the writer was oblivious about? How art critics create narratives that would perplex the artist? Similarly, someone else might find a good narrative in your academic work that you had not even consciously realised. Given some distance, your colleagues can often see the wood, when all that you can see are the individual trees.

This doesn't always happen in time for your promotion application unfortunately. In my case it certainly didn't. But I do have two good examples that occurred after my promotion to Full Professor. In 2015, the book "*Grands Auteurs en Management International*" devoted a full chapter to my contributions to the field of International Business. The authors of the chapter saw a logic in my research programmes that I had not consciously realised, and documented explicitly how it influenced the field.

Harzing's work offers a strong contribution by virtue of its integration into the core field of international management [...]. First of all, she adopted a logic of testing and extending previous research (Harzing, 2000; Harzing and Noorderhaven, 2006a), especially at the start of her career. In addition, her typology of modes of control (Harzing, 1999) was taken up by many researchers and has profoundly influenced the literature on coordination and control mechanisms.

Her reflections on expatriation, and in particular the question of the failure rate for expatriation (Harzing, 1995, 2002), have strongly influenced international HR researchers. Her work on the influence of the country-of-origin and the questioning of the European MNC model (Harzing and Sorge, 2003; Harzing, Sorge and Paauwe, 2002; Harzing and Noorderhaven, 2008) was likewise pioneering. It is interesting to note contributions with long-term co-authors, on the same themes, which contributed to a powerful cumulative narrative logic.

Earlier, in 2011, Stephen Bensman's review of my Publish or Perish book and his assessment of me as a "woman with an agenda" was completely unexpected. But yes, he was absolutely right!

My involvement in the area of bibliometrics and the creation of the Publish or Perish software (see screenshot above) was driven by a strong drive to democratise access to research evaluation and to change the playing field for Social scientists.

I must say I loved the bit at the end of the review where he compared the Publish or Perish software to a *"torpedo blasting paths through the evaluative defenses surrounding the entrenched positions of academia"*. It is the closest that I ever got to being a revolutionary!

> Anne-Wil Harzing is a woman with an agenda. To understand this agenda, you have to know that she is a Professor of International Management at the University of Melbourne, Australia. The discipline of management is a social science, which is as vocational as it is academic. In the United States such disciplines—including, for example, business administration, education, law, library and information science, social work, etc.—are evaluated separately from the academic disciplines, because they operate on different principles and literature bases than academic disciplines in the humanities, social sciences, and—particularly—the sciences.
>
> Harzing's agenda was set forth in a joint article she did with Nancy J. Adler, a management professor at McGill University, Montreal, Canada. In this article Adler and Harzing (2009) argue that current systems of academically ranking institutions and individuals are dysfunctional and counterproductive. Moreover, due to institutional isomorphism, the same systems are being adopted everywhere, leading to the following situation: "Dominant institutional players form what is referred to as a well-organized field in which each player is influenced to adhere to similar, mutually reinforcing types of ranking and assessment behaviors" (p. 85). One way to reform such a system is through the introduction of what Adler and Harzing describe as "a new and influential field-level player—what has been labeled an institutional entrepreneur" (p. 90). Anne-Wil Harzing is such an entrepreneur.

The winning combination

The winning combination is a great narrative which exudes passion, combined with concrete evidence of impact. One without the other is difficult to sell, having neither is a sure-fire way to fail. Many promotion applications are dry and disjointed summaries reporting that *"I have done this, this, and this"* without evidence of impact. Sometimes they are supplemented by an implicit or explicit threat *"by the way my promotion is long overdue, and you'd better promote me or else..."*. They lack both a coherent narrative and substantive evidence.

Your promotion panel should get a feel for your academic *identity* and academic passion. They don't want to see a cardboard cut-out academic, slotting into a standard template. Although it might not always feel like it, they are not looking for a person that just "ticks the boxes". Who are you? What makes you tick? What do you stand for? Their hearts should be swelling with pride for having such a great colleague. They shouldn't be falling asleep when wrestling through a tedious record of roles, or getting annoyed by baseless bragging without evidence.

In its new promotion guidelines, Middlesex University explicitly asks applicants to reflect on their academic identity before setting out their case for promotion:

> *"Briefly reflect on the motivation for the activities in which you have been involved and your overarching goals, principles and values."*

Pro tip: link your narrative to your university's mission

This shows you engage with the university outside your own department, which is crucial for career progression to senior levels. Yes, I know strategy documents can often appear contrived and vacuous. But they do tell you *something* about your university's key values and priorities. Is it mainly focused on teaching and learning, or does it seem to prioritise research? Is its focus on fundamental research or more applied research? How important is engagement with external stakeholders?

For instance, Middlesex University's purpose is to *"create knowledge and put it into action to develop fairer, healthier, more prosperous and sustainable societies"*. Referring to its Latin motto *"rerum cognoscere causas"*, LSE's purpose and vision is to be *"a community of people and ideas, founded to know the causes of things, for the betterment of society"*. Their ultimate focus is not worlds apart, but the emphases are quite different.

In 2022 Middlesex University completely revamped its promotion criteria. In addition to explicitly including collegiality as one of its criteria, it also made the link to its mission more explicit:

> *"Strategy 2031 presents our vision and aims for the future, our values and what we value. It is important that our promotion and progression align with our shared values and the process reflects the focus on collegiality, as well as a continued commitment to equality, diversity and inclusivity."*

Finally: see it as time for reflection

Does even just reading this make you feel tired? I am not surprised. But don't forget that this series is meant to be a distillation of "best practice". Don't feel you have to *all* that is listed above to be successful in your promotion application. You don't have to be a superhero (see my blogpost *"We need a different kind of superhero: improving gender diversity in academia"*).

That said, writing up a good case for promotion does take time. It took me more than a month full-time to put my first one together, though partly that's because in most Australian universities the case runs to twenty pages. I won't lie, I did curse the time I had to spend on promotion applications. I was promoted internally to Associate and full Professor and was rejected the first time, so I have had to spend several months of my research time on this.

However, ultimately, I am grateful that I was "forced" to put in the work. It really made me think about my academic career and where I wanted to go. It led directly to a major change in how I represented my research programs and argued my contribution to my discipline. It also made me more aware of the metrics that are used to evaluate academic performance. This came in very handy in my new role as Associate Dean Research at the University of Melbourne, and later in my roles as Research Mentor and Staff Development Lead at Middlesex University.

So, try to see work on your promotion application not as a "chore" in which you need to comply with silly rules or as a battle with organisational politics. Instead, see it as an investment in yourself to help you really articulate what you are proud of and how you would like to spend the next 5, 10, or 15 years of your academic career.

Finally, remember you can reuse your carefully crafted promotion statements in lots of other settings: funding applications, applications for academic awards or fellowships, yearly performance appraisals, applying for external promotion. Heck, you can even use them nearly 20 years after the fact to write up blogposts and a book about promotion applications ☺.

Chapter 7: Internal versus external promotion

Most academics will tell you that external promotion – getting promoted by applying for a higher-level job at another institution – is a lot "easier" than internal promotion – getting promoted by putting in a promotion application at your own institution.

For one thing, it is generally *much* less work. My own – internal – promotion applications at the University of Melbourne took me six weeks of work to prepare. They were substantive 20-page documents in which you needed to make an "argued case" that you were already operating at the level that you wanted to be promoted to.

In terms of research, this means more than simply listing grants, publications, and citations. You are expected to show your "leadership in the academic discipline", which involves having a coherent research program (or preferably several programs; I had five active research programs when I applied as Associate Professor) that has made a real difference in the field, both academically and societally.

So rather than just rattling off the mantra "I have 15 A*/4* and 10 A/3* – or whatever the ranking system is – publications", you need to talk about why the actual *content* of your research has made a real difference and is of major international significance. This is something many academics find surprisingly hard to do!

In contrast, applying for promotion externally can be as simple as sending in your CV and a short application letter, or even just being headhunted for a particular position. At worst, it might involve struggling with online application systems and addressing specific selection criteria, but in my – admittedly limited – experience, this rarely takes more than a day or two.

However, in addition to being more time-consuming, internal promotion is also typically harder to achieve. The same academic record that might see you rejected for promotion internally might well lead to an offer for external promotion. It is therefore not surprising that many academics take the external route and come back to their home institution with a job offer, expecting it to be matched.

In some countries, universities even actively encourage this. They are unwilling to consider promotion, or a salary raise unless academics secure an outside offer. Some academics even told me that handing in your notice (i.e., resigning) might grant you "instant promotion". Although these strategies might well work, they are by no means guaranteed to do so. So be prepared to walk away or eat humble pie!

In the rest of this chapter, I will explain why external promotion is generally easier, but also why there might well be some advantages to internal promotion too.

Seven reasons why external promotion is easier

There are at least seven reasons why internal promotion is less likely to be successful than external promotion. Not all of these will apply in every institution or for every individual application, but I think you will find that at least a couple of them are likely to be relevant to your case.

Please note that I am not saying that these seven reasons are necessarily *good* reasons or that I would defend (all of) them; I am simply *describing* the *reality* of what I see happening in academia.

1. Different incentive structures

If you apply for an external position, the university has a job vacancy. This means they have a *gap* in their department, and they *really want* to appoint someone, whether to improve research standing, increase their grant income, cover specific classes, or take on that role as Head of Department or Associate Dean that nobody else wants to do.

This means that they are very likely to err on the side of appointing someone, even if the candidate might not be 100% adequate. I have been on committees where our choice was between appointing an 70-80% candidate or going "back to the market" for yet another time-consuming round of recruitment and 6-12 months delay, without any firm guarantee that we would get better applicants.

When you apply for internal promotion, your university is already enjoying all the advantages of having you as an employee. They are not really going to get anything "extra" by promoting you. The best they can look forward to is a happier employee (or at least one who isn't angry, frustrated, and hurt by being rejected). However, even these "happy feelings" will wear off after a few months; we quickly get used to better circumstances.

If your employer is lucky, they can ask you to take on an unpopular job that only people at a certain level can or are allowed to do. Mostly though, they just need to pay you more! Not much more in most cases, I agree, but with university budgets as squeezed as they are, promoting just a dozen people to (Associate) Professor might be a significant addition to the wage bill. So, the incentive structures for internal and external promotion are entirely different.

2. Two vs a dozen criteria

In research-intensive universities external promotions focus on your publication and grant record. Yes, they want to know that you won't have students running away screaming from your lectures. Yes, they want to see *some* service to the academic community and – depending on the level – *some* administrative experience or leadership.

However, just showing your teaching evaluations are ok, having done some reviewing or editorial work, and having been chair of a program or – if you are very junior – having been part some committees is usually sufficient. Typically, it is all about your research.

Compare that with internal promotions. Even for teaching alone you need to show you have "transformed students' lives", have introduced teaching innovations, consistently taught according to the 7, 8, 9, 10, 11, 12, 13 or even 20 "principles of effective teaching" and/or embodied the "values of the university" through your teaching.

And we haven't even started yet on service, knowledge transfer and leadership. So, rather than being evaluated on just two key metrics – publications and grants – you are often evaluated on at least a dozen, including your ability to write persuasively. Clearly this presents a higher risk of rejection.

3. Strengths and weaknesses

Whether you apply internally or externally, you will always try to play to your strengths. However, if you apply internally your colleagues know much more about you than when you apply externally. Your research achievements are usually easy to judge "objectively". Hence in external promotion applications, research achievements will be noticed quite easily. However, weaknesses are not as easy to spot by perusing a CV or even by interviewing the candidate. Unlike in industry, the question: "what are your weaknesses" is not often asked in academic interviews and even if it was, it is easy to prepare a stock answer to that.

Internally, people know both your strengths and your weaknesses; the overall balance might work out more negatively than externally. Even worse, academic achievements might be known and appreciated more widely by an external appointment committee (that is more likely to be composed of *experts* in the field) than by an internal committee (that often includes many academics *outside the discipline*). I have yet to meet the first research-oriented academic who doesn't feel they are appreciated more outside their institution than inside ☺.

4. Comparison against past, current, and future applications

Internal promotion usually means that your case is compared against colleagues who have, or have not, been promoted to the same level in order not to disrupt the internal "ecosystem" of the department/university. You will also be compared to others who are going up for promotion at the same time. Even though all of you might meet the "objective" standards (which usually aren't that clear in any case), it is unlikely the University will be able to afford to promote everyone. Some universities have a fixed number of places, especially for senior levels.

You might even be compared to "future" applicants in the context of "not wanting to set a precedent". Promotion panels know that if they let *one* person through with, for instance, fewer publications at a certain level than they would normally expect, but with a better record on less visible aspects of the job or with particularly scarce skills in another area, they can expect a deluge of applicants the next year who will try to "push the boundary" just that little bit further.

Obviously, comparative performance is important for external promotions too, but you are compared primarily with the other external job applicants. If you are applying for a job that – for whatever reason – few people have applied for, this "comparison set" might be fairly small.

Of course, your prospective new colleagues sitting on the selection committee will compare you to internal candidates as well. They won't appreciate having someone appointed to a particular level with a weaker academic record than they or their close colleagues had when they were rejected for internal promotion. However, they typically do not know your academic record as well as that of their internal colleagues. Their verdict might also be "sweetened" by the fact that at least they get a reduction in their workload by appointing a new staff member.

5. Internal relationships

Although both internal and external promotion applications need to be supported by external referees, internal promotions are ultimately decided by a committee of internal academics. This means that internal relationships might play a role. The importance of relationships is by no means absent in external appointments, but there is less of a "web of relationships" than there is in your own institution.

As I argued in several other points, internal promotion committees generally "err on the conservative side" i.e., if there is any doubt of the candidate's credentials, they will generally reject the application. Hence, they might well reject an internal application even if only one (influential) panel member is not supportive.

You might well be the nicest colleague in the world, but after having worked in an institution for some time, you (or your supporters!) are likely to have made *some* "enemies". And remember that it is not just you who is being evaluated; it is also the Head of Department or School supporting you, or even the discipline you are working in!

6. A hierarchy of levels

Internal promotions typically go through several rounds of decisions. For (Associate) Professor it is not unusual to have to go through a Department, School or Faculty, and University committee. Not only does this create three hurdles instead of the single hurdle you have to cross with external promotions, but it also increases the likelihood of some level of internal competition playing a role.

> *"Why is the Department of Management getting support for three promotions again, isn't it time for the Department of Finance got one?" "Why do we promote people in the Business School, they already get paid way more than us Philosophers anyway?" "Why would I promote this candidate supported by Professor X who was so negative about "my" candidate before?"*

I am not at all suggesting these deliberations take place openly (they almost never do) or even that they are frequent. But they may make a difference, especially if you are only performing at 100% or 110% of the expectations, not 150%. Having your application evaluated above the Departmental level also increases the risk of people outside the discipline judging your performance according to their own disciplinary standards.

> *"We in [Chemistry, Micro-biology, Astrophysics ...] publish at least a dozen articles a year, surely one or two articles a year cannot be sufficient for promotion?"*

As Associate Dean Research in a Faculty of Economics and Business I had to fight a similar battle at an aggregate level every single year at our Faculty's Strategic Performance Review, having to explain that doubling our publication output would mean that we would outperform Harvard and MIT by a very substantial margin.

7. A self-perpetuating rite of passage

The internal promotion process is partly a self-perpetuating process of mutual torture. As I have explained above, internal promotion is generally more difficult to achieve than promotion through external routes.

So, everyone who has gone through the internal process has had at least one rejection or bad experience under his or her belt. Or even if they haven't, they might have had a close friend who had. As a result, many academics might reason:

> *"I [my friend] have suffered even though I [she] had a great case, so why should this colleague get an easy run?"*

I fully agree that this is not a particularly nice or rational reaction, but remember: academics are human too. They might even think it is character building to reject you first time around!

In sum

So, do I recommend you to apply for promotion outside your own institution? No, not necessarily. As I will discuss in the next section, for all its faults there are some areas in which internal promotion might trump external promotion.

So yes, apply for a job externally if you think the job, the university or the country would suit you better. Or if after 5, 10 or 15 years at an institution you really want a change. But I would caution you against applying externally if your *primary* aim is to be promoted a year or two earlier than you might be internally.

Seven advantages of internal promotion

The previous section might have given the impression that external promotion is by far the preferred option. However, I by no means think that is always true. Below, I provide several reasons why going for internal promotion might have considerable advantages too.

In the spirit of balance, I have also come up with seven points in this section. You are unlikely to agree with all my arguments, but I think you will find that at least a couple of them are likely to be relevant to your case.

1. Rewards a balanced academic record

I argued above that external promotion might be easier as it typically focuses on a limited number of criteria. In case of a research-oriented position, this might be mainly publications and research funding. As such, this may well reward academics who excel in these aspects of an academic job, whilst not necessarily being terribly strong in other aspects such as teaching, leadership, and external engagement.

However, as a direct corollary, this means that internal promotion might be an "easier" route if you have a more balanced academic profile. If you are a very good, but not stellar researcher, combined with a profile that includes a significant, but not stellar, contribution to teaching or university leadership you might find the internal route easier than applying externally.

2. Improves persuasion skills

Internal promotion teaches you how to make a persuasive case about your academic record much better than external promotions do. This is particularly true in academic systems where internal promotion applications consist of a substantive argued case about your leadership in the discipline, teaching, and university management.

For my promotion applications to both Associate and Full Professor in Australia, I had to submit a very densely argued 20-page case that evidenced – amongst many other things – that my research programs were coherent and of major international significance, that I had an international reputation, and that I had played a significant role in leading research projects and mentoring junior colleagues.

The preparation of these applications took up well over two months of my research time and at the time I hated the fact that I had to go through it. However, I have been able to draw on the materials that I was forced to prepare for my promotion applications ever since. For me, it has also led directly to a major change in how I represented my research programs and argued my contribution to my discipline.

Now there might well be other, less painful, ways to improve your persuasion skills, but being "forced" to make your case this for your internal promotion is not all bad. For me, the newly acquired skills came in very handy when making my case for funding applications, applications for fellowships, as well as other types of awards.

3. Strengths and weaknesses

In the previous section on external promotion, I argued that weaknesses in your academic record might be less apparent in external promotions. But remember that just like individuals, institutions have strengths and weakness too. If you apply for external promotion, your new institution is going to present *only* their strengths, *not* their weaknesses.

So, the grass might well *appear* greener at another institution. You will only discover your new institution's weaknesses after having started to work there. "Better the Devil you know..." and "Out of the frying pan into the fire" are other proverbs that come to mind here.

Unless you have close friends inside the new institution, nobody will tell you about weaknesses such as the department bully that, for one reason or another, is protected or tolerated, or the department's long history of employment disputes or sexual harassment.

You may well find that the promises that were made during the job interview evaporate in the daily realities of the job, even if they were written into your contract. Or you may find that this "guaranteed" high level of conference funding – a key thing that attracted you to the new job – is axed only two years later, leaving you with less than you had at your current institution.

4. More productivity, less stress

Internal promotion avoids the "transaction cost" associated with moving to another institution. The actual level of these transaction costs depends on whether the move also involves moving home or even countries. It also makes a difference whether you are a young academic unencumbered by family obligations or whether you are part of a dual career couple, have children at school age, or aging parents who need care. However, any move leads to a reduced level of productivity and an increased level of stress for a certain period.

5. Avoids being dumped upon

New external recruits often end up with the worst classes or the worst administrative jobs. Your Head of Department and your new colleagues will reason that you need to take on new classes or jobs anyway so they might as well give you the classes or jobs they don't want to do.

Although it is not at all uncommon to be asked to do "unpopular" jobs after being promoted internally, you are often in a better position to avoid them. For one thing, knowing the institution better you can more easily recognize them!

6. Avoids resentment

In external promotions you are appointed at a specific academic level by the selection panel. However, unless it is abundantly obvious that you are in fact fully qualified for this level, you might face a backlash. You may find your appointment has left some of your new colleagues – especially those who haven't been involved in the decision-making – resentful. They might well have applied for the same level internally with a better record than you had and have been rejected.

This is not a particularly pleasant work climate to be in and it will hinder any collaborative relationships with your new colleagues. Now you might be a person that doesn't particularly care about any of this, or who prefers to work with outside colleagues anyway. Even so, there are few people who wouldn't prefer friendly colleagues to colleagues who actively resent and avoid you.

7. Maintains good relationships

In situations where, when taking up an external job, you have left your old institution unexpectedly, with very short notice, or after working there for only a short time, your old colleagues might not be too happy about this. As in any other workplace, relationships matter in academia.

But unlike in workplaces outside academia, these old colleagues might well be the ones evaluating your grant application, fellowship application, or be an acting editor on one of your papers when you submit them to a journal. In contrast, if you have finally "battled your way" through internal promotion, your colleagues will generally be very happy for you and appreciate you even more.

Some final tips for promotion applications

If you do go for promotion, whether it is internal or external, these tips and reflections might be useful to help you navigate the process.

The past is another country...

Please note that promotion requirements differ by university, by country, by rank, and over time. Some countries might not even have an internal promotion route to Full Professor. Take your time to get familiar with what is valued at your university. Learn to distinguish which academic achievements are universal and which are country specific. Most of all, try to accept that *"the past is another country: they do things differently there"*.

Yes, I know that there are (Associate) Professors at your institution or the external institution that you are applying to that don't meet all the criteria you now need to fulfil to get promoted or appointed. Some might not even have a PhD. How do I know? Because they are there at every institution. They were certainly there at every single one of the six universities I have worked for. Performance criteria do change over time, but so does access to resources: try doing a PhD without access to the internet or even email. Yes, I am that old ☺.

Please also realise that you can almost never compare yourself directly to other academics as so many of us do when our applications are rejected. *"But I am so much better than so-and-so, I have more ..."* What you don't know, or what you conveniently ignore, is that you might well have *much* less of something else.

Having seen dozens of internal promotion applications I have *always* been surprised and often humbled by what my colleagues had done. There is much more to an academic record than can be gleaned from a 1-minute glance through their list of publications. Moreover, we typically only compare ourselves to those in higher ranks who we *think* have done less, ignoring those at the same or lower rank who have done much more.

Don't let university politics ruin your sanity

Of course, in some cases there might be "political" reasons for why someone wasn't promoted or appointed at an external institution. I feel I have suffered from university politics at several junctures in my career and it has kept me awake at night more than once. However, this happens to most academics at some stage in their career, it seems to be inevitable wherever human beings work together. Academic life can be very unfair. What I am saying is not to focus on this *too* much, as it only makes the effects of it worse.

For what it is worth, my experience has been that those rejected for internal promotion whilst having a good case are generally promoted in the next round. Although it might seem it is taking forever to get to then next academic level, many good academics will spend by far the largest chunk of their career at an Associate or Full professorial level. Please see a 1–2-year delay in that perspective. By all means, do fight systematic injustice – as I have done in several institutions – but don't let it "eat you up". Try and redirect your energy.

Apply early rather than late

Unless you think you are unable to cope with being rejected (whether for internal or external promotion), apply as soon as you think you stand *any* chance of being accepted. Women in particular typically wait far too long to apply for promotion, often waiting until they meet all the requirements for 150%, whereas men oftentimes apply as soon as they meet just *one* of the requirements.

Given that promotion applications are often considered in the context of what you have done since your last promotion, consistently being promoted 1-3 years "too late" can add up over an entire career. You cannot easily catch up after one late promotion.

Moreover, by applying for promotion you ensure that you get a clear-cut signal about what your chances are. And rather than guessing, in the case of an internal promotion you are often given feedback about what you need to do to be successful next time. If your university doesn't offer this feedback automatically, ask for it and then refer back to it very specifically when you apply again! This is how I did this in my second application for promotion to full Professor.

Letter to the Faculty Committee,

My 2006 promotion application was not allowed to go forward to the University Promotions Committee. In my feedback session with Prof. XXX, I was informed that I was "doing all the right things" but needed one more big publication hit OR a couple of smaller hits OR a substantial increase in citations OR something of equivalent standing.

As I will argue below, I have done not just one, but **all** of these things and more last year. I received **two acceptances** in a top management journal and **two revise & resubmits** in top management journals. My citations increased by nearly 100 in the last year alone. I was selected as Departmental Editor Culture and Cognition for JIBS, the top journal in my field. I also significantly expanded my service to the academic community by providing a free software programme "Publish or Perish", which is available for download at www.harzing.com. Finally, I was headhunted for a Chair in IHRM at Reading University, the top British university in International Business, an offer that I declined to stay in Australia. The letter below provides more details of my achievements in the last year. The application itself has been revised.

Conclusion

In Chapter 1, I explained why universities promote academics and how you can make a head start to develop a successful promotion application. In Chapter 2, I showed you how to use your experience with the process of submitting an article for publication to understand the requirements for promotion applications.

In the next three chapters, I demonstrated how you can create a well-argued case for each of the three core aspects of an academic job by demonstrating your impact: Research & Engagement (Chapter 3), Teaching & Learning (Chapter 4), and finally Leadership & Service (Chapter 5).

Subsequently, in Chapter 6, I showed how having a coherent statement of your academic identity can turn your application from a fairly sterile list of achievements into a compelling career narrative. Finally, in Chapter 7, I explained why internal promotion is often harder to achieve than external promotion.

I hope this book has helped you to better understand the background to this highly contested topic and provide you with the tools to be successful in your own promotion application. I wish you all the very best in your own promotion application. I would also love to hear from you if this book has helped you; feel free to get in touch with me at anne@harzing.com.

Further reading

My blog contains many more posts related to academic promotions, as well as academic careers more generally. Below I have reproduced a partial list structured by topic. Just Google the title and you will find them easily.

Career progression

CYGNA: Internal versus External promotion
11 Oct 2018 - Anne-Wil Harzing
Reports on our 22nd CYGNA meeting with a presentation giving tips for internal and external promotion applications

CYGNA: climbing up the academic career ladder
03 May 2021 - Anne-Wil Harzing
Reports on our 39th CYGNA meeting with a focus on career progression

CYGNA: How do I keep my job (in academia) in uncertain times?
13 Nov 2020 - Anne-Wil Harzing
Reports on our 34th CYGNA meeting discussing jobs losses in higher education in COVID-19 times

CYGNA: One size doesn't fit all - Diversity of academic career paths
28 Feb 2022 - Anne-Wil Harzing
Reports on our 45th CYGNA meeting in which we discussed four alternative career paths in academia

Open Syllabus Explorer: evidencing research-based teaching?
15 Nov 2019 - Anne-Wil Harzing
Reviews how the Open Syllabus Project can help academics to understand their impact on teaching and find the best textbook for their course

Presenting your case for tenure or promotion?
23 Nov 2016 - Anne-Wil Harzing
Shows how to make your case for tenure or promotion by comparing your record to a relevant peer group

How to create a sustainable academic career
21 Nov 2020 - Anne-Wil Harzing
Reports on Martyna Sliwa's presentation on career progression in the UK higher education environment

How to create a successful academic career: AIB - Ask, Invest & Believe
22 Jun 2019 - Anne-Wil Harzing
Write-up of my contribution to a conference panel on career strategies at the 2017 AIB-UKI meeting in Birmingham

CV of failures
15 Jun 2019 - Anne-Wil Harzing
Explains why rejection and failure are a normal part of an academic career and not something to hide or be embarrassed about

Publish or Perish increases transparency in academic appointments
14 Oct 2016 - Anne-Wil Harzing
Illustrates how PoP has been used to expose nepotism and incompetence

CYGNA: Careers, mobility and belonging: foreign women academics in the UK
02 Jun 2018 - Anne-Wil Harzing
Reports on our 15th CYGNA meeting with a special emphasis on the challenges for female foreign academics in the UK

Why are there so few female Economics professors?
11 Nov 2018 - Anne-Wil Harzing
Short summary of my article in Economisch Statistische Berichten on gender bias and meritocracy in academia

We need a different kind of superhero: improving gender diversity in academia
12 Jan 2021 - Jill A. Gould
Collects the resources developed for the 2020 AoM symposium on creating gender inclusive academic environments

WAIB Panel: Academic career strategies for women in the UK
01 May 2018 - Anne-Wil Harzing
Reports on a WAIB Panel at the AIB-UKI meeting in Birmingham April 2018

Publishing

The four P's of getting published
08 Dec 2016 - Anne-Wil Harzing
Short summary of my white paper explaining how performance, practice, participation, and persistence are needed to publish academic papers

The four ailments of academic writing and how to cure them
20 Apr 2020 - Nico Pizzolato
Some golden tips on how to improve your academic writing

How to keep up-to-date with the literature, but avoid information overload?
14 May 2018 - Anne-Wil Harzing
Provides tips on how to keep up-to-date without getting lost

How to avoid a desk-reject in seven steps [1/8]
10 May 2020 - Anne-Wil Harzing
Introduces a 7-step process to increase your chances of getting your paper into the review process

Who do you want to talk to? Targeting journals [2/8]
24 May 2020 - Anne-Wil Harzing
Explains why choosing your target journal is the most important step in the publication process

Your title: the public face of your paper [3/8]
14 Jun 2020 - Anne-Wil Harzing
Illustrates how to create a good title through an iterative process

Writing your abstract: not a last-minute activity [4/8]
28 Jun 2020 - Anne-Wil Harzing
Explains what needs to be included in an effective abstract

Your introduction: first impressions count! [5/8]
11 Sep 2020 - Anne-Wil Harzing
What are the elements of an effective introduction: context, importance and interest

Conclusions: last impressions count too! [6/8]
18 Sep 2020 - Anne-Wil Harzing
Why conclusions are a crucial part of your paper's key message

What do you cite? Using references strategically [7/8]
03 Oct 2020 - Anne-Wil Harzing
Shows you how references can save you hundreds of words and position your paper

Why do I need to write a letter to the editor? [8/8]
16 Oct 2020 - Anne-Wil Harzing
The last step in the submission process is an important means to "sell" your paper to the journal

From little seed to fully-grown tree: a paper development journey
09 May 2022 - Heejin Kim
A novice publisher providing a "behind the scenes" look at co-authoring for top journals

Want to publish a literature review? Think of it as an empirical paper
23 Apr 2021 - Tatiana Andreeva
What to consider if you want to publish a literature review paper

CYGNA: The wonderful world of book publishing
12 Dec 2020 - Anne-Wil Harzing
Reports on our 35th CYGNA meeting with three publishers discussing textbooks, research books and practice books

CYGNA: Writing a literature review paper: whether, what, and when?
19 Sep 2021 - Anne-Wil Harzing
Reports on our 41st CYGNA meeting on the challenge of publishing literature review papers

Own your place in the world by writing a book
11 Dec 2018 - Nico Pizzolato
A passionate plea to consider publishing a book at least once in your academic career

IB Frontline interview: mentoring section
03 Jan 2022 - Anne-Wil Harzing
Introduces the third section of my IB Frontline interview talking about my role as a mentor and my top tips for early career researchers

Research impact and funding

The four C's of getting cited
18 Sep 2017 - Anne-Wil Harzing
Short summary of white paper explaining why competence, collaboration, care and communication help to realise the citation impact of your work

Everything you always wanted to know about impact...
02 Jun 2019 - Anne-Wil Harzing
Book chapter providing a quick overview of the what, why, how and where of research impact

Impact is impact is impact? Well, no...
20 Jun 2022 - Anne-Wil Harzing
Reprint of an invited blogpost on the SAGE Social Science Space on disambiguating the concept of impact

How to make your case for impact?

13 Jul 2016 - Anne-Wil Harzing

Shows you how to make your case for impact by comparing your papers to the journal average

Research Academics as Change Makers - Opportunities and Barriers

13 Nov 2021 - Andrea Werner

Reports on a Middlesex University panel discussion on creating external research impact

Making your case for impact if you have few citations

27 Nov 2017 - Anne-Wil Harzing

Provides advice on strategies to demonstrate impact with a very low citation level

How to ensure your paper achieves the impact it deserves?

15 Jan 2018 - Anne-Wil Harzing

Discusses the workflow I use to communicate about a new paper

How to find your next research project?

16 Jun 2016 - Anne-Wil Harzing

Provides suggestions on how to find new and interesting research projects

CYGNA: Working in a Horizon-2020 project

19 Feb 2021 - Anne-Wil Harzing

Reports on our 37th CYGNA meeting dealing with research funding and working in large, funded projects

How to write successful funding applications?

02 Nov 2016 - Anne-Wil Harzing

Provides ten tips for successful funding applications

CYGNA: Positionality, team roles, and academic activism

27 Jun 2022 - Anne-Wil Harzing

Reports on our 47th CYGNA meeting, celebrating our 8-year anniversary with our first face-to-face meeting in 2.5 years

Social media

Social Media in Academia (1): Introduction
16 Jan 2020 - Anne-Wil Harzing
An introduction into my 8-part blogpost series on social media

Social Media in Academia (2): Comparing the options
28 Jan 2020 - Anne-Wil Harzing
General recommendations on how to use social media professionally

Social Media in Academia (3): Google Scholar Profiles
10 Feb 2020 - Anne-Wil Harzing
Provides recommendations on how to get the best out of Google Scholar Profiles

Social Media in Academia (4): LinkedIn
27 Feb 2020 - Anne-Wil Harzing
Provides recommendations on how to get the best out of LinkedIn

Social media in Academia (5): ResearchGate
09 Mar 2020 - Anne-Wil Harzing
Provides recommendations on how to get the most out of ResearchGate

Social Media in Academia (6): Twitter
27 Mar 2020 - Anne-Wil Harzing
Provides recommendations on how to get the best out of Twitter

Social media in Academia (7): Blogging
13 Apr 2020 - Anne-Wil Harzing
Provides recommendations on how to start with blogging

Social Media in Academia (8): Putting it all together
27 Apr 2020 - Anne-Wil Harzing
Final posting in the social media series explains how different social media can reinforce each other

Social Media in Academia: Using LinkedIn to promote your research
08 Apr 2021 - Christa Sathish
Tips and tricks for using LinkedIn to promote your research

How to digitally market yourself: a beginner's guide for students and academics
06 Nov 2021 - Christa Sathish
Handy tips and tricks to start building a digital presence

Other academic skills

Be proactive, resilient & realistic!
07 Jan 2020 - Anne-Wil Harzing
Argues that as an academic you are an independent professional shaping your own career

How to prevent burn-out? About staying sane in academia
12 May 2016 - Anne-Wil Harzing
Provides twelve suggestions on how to prevent burn-out and keep your sanity

CYGNA: Work intensification, well-being and career advancement
08 Dec 2019 - Anne-Wil Harzing
Reports on our 29th CYGNA meeting dealing with workloads and work intensification

On academic life: collaborations and active engagement
19 Jun 2018 - Anne-Wil Harzing
Discusses Martyna Sliwa's articles on the different rationalities underlying research collaborations and the need to get involved in managing and shaping the university organisations we work for

Want to impress at an academic job interview?
24 Jan 2017 - Anne-Wil Harzing
Shows you how to use PoP do some intelligence gathering to make a good impression at a job interview

CYGNA: Working effectively with support staff in academia
06 Mar 2018 - Anne-Wil Harzing
Reports on our 18th CYGNA meeting on working with support staff and a discussion of boundaryless careers

CYGNA: Life-long learning in academia
03 Apr 2019 - Anne-Wil Harzing
Reports on our 25th CYGNA meeting with presentations on an Erasmus visit and participation in the Aurora program

How to hold on to your sanity in academia
11 Apr 2019 - Steffi Siegert
Steffi Siegert's powerful contribution that sums up everything that women can be facing in academia

CYGNA: Negotiation workshop
15 Feb 2020 - Anne-Wil Harzing
Reports on our 30th CYGNA meeting dealing with negotiation styles

How to promote your research achievements without being obnoxious?
01 Dec 2018 - Anne-Wil Harzing
Provides some quick and easy to implement tips on how to promote your academic work

CYGNA: Resistance to gender equality in academia
15 Mar 2021 - Anne-Wil Harzing
Reports on our 38th CYGNA meeting dealing with one of the ultimate gender topics

What is that conference networking thing all about?
01 Nov 2017 - Anne-Wil Harzing
Reflections on the importance of networking in academia and tips on how to do it

CYGNA: Supervising and being supervised
02 May 2022 - Anne-Wil Harzing
Reports on our 46th CYGNA meeting where we discussed our experiences of PhD supervision, both from a student and from a supervisor perspective

Appendix: Example of promotion application, full professor

On the next pages you will find a copy of the first 18 pages of my own promotion application to professor at the University of Melbourne in 2007. This was the first section of this application and was followed by a section with my nominated referees, a section with future plans for research and teaching, an abbreviated CV and a full list of publications.

This application was successful, after an unsuccessful application the year before. Note this application was created for a specific academic system, the Australian system, and more in particular for one of the Go8 universities, which is Australia's group of top universities. Hence, expectations regarding publications were fairly high.

That said, this application is now more than 15 years old. This means that the specific level of metrics such as citations and journal impact factors are substantially lower than would be expected currently, with many metrics having doubled, tripled, or even quadrupled. This is caused by both a significant expansion of database coverage and a very significant increase in publications (and thus potential for citations) over the last two decades.

Moreover, developments regarding the importance of societal impact were still in their infancy and only recognised in the most progressive universities. Likewise, the emphasis on coherent career narratives was still far in the future. Hence, please do not see this as a model of what current applications should look like.

However, the general framing and rhetoric style of the application is largely timeless. So, I hope it will be useful to you to have an extended example. You are more than welcome to borrow and adapt any phrases, comparisons, or rhetoric styles that are useful to your case without asking for my permission. I wish you all the best with your own promotion application!

LETTER OF APPLICATION

This letter forms part of my application to promotion to Level E (Professor). In it I will argue that I have achieved and sustained a distinguished record in scholarship, teaching and service to the University and wider academic community.

- **Research**: Since joining the University of Melbourne, I have consolidated and further enhanced my international scholarly reputation in my academic discipline, International Management. The quality of my research is evidenced by the journals in which I publish, many of which are the top international journals in their respective fields. The large number of citations to my work (289 in the Social Science Citation Index, and many more in non-ISI journals, research books and conference papers) demonstrates its substantial impact. In the six years since joining Melbourne, I have published twenty-one refereed journal articles (+ five in press), one book and five book chapters (+ two in press), and produced fourteen published and twenty-two unpublished refereed conference papers. More than half of this output was realised since my promotion to Associate Professor. I have also secured a University grant and two Faculty grants, as well as a $185,000 ARC Discovery grant.

- **Teaching**: My teaching activities are wide in scope and high in quality. In my time with the University I have taught seven different subjects, all of which were either fully or partially newly developed. My teaching evaluations are excellent, and verbal and written feedback shows a very high level of satisfaction with both the content and style of my teaching.

- **Service**: I have taken every opportunity to be of service to the University and have performed a range of committee functions at Departmental, Faculty and University level. I am director of the PhD program in the Department of Management. My academic web site is seen as a major resource site for the research community in International Management, and is further evidence of my service to the University as well as to the academic discipline. In addition, I play an active role in my academic discipline through my extensive work as mentor of junior colleagues, as reviewer, editorial board member and associate editor, and through committee leadership in Academy of Management.

I therefore propose that my performance shows a sustained record of achievement that is consistent with the standards of a Level E academic. The remainder of this document supports my application based on the criteria set forth in the guidelines for promotion to professor.

LEADERSHIP IN MY ACADEMIC DISCIPLINE

Since starting my academic career in the early 1990s, I have been passionately interested in all aspects of International Management. My research has spanned several sub-disciplines within this area: comparative management, international business strategy, international human resource management and cross-cultural management. With the globalisation of the world economy and the increasing importance of multinational companies (MNCs), research in this area is of crucial importance. My own research has focused on two broad areas. First, how do MNCs manage their foreign subsidiaries (including their HRM practices) to realise their objectives of global efficiency, local responsiveness and worldwide learning? Second, how do (American) theories of management need to be adapted when they are applied across borders? Management of cultural and language differences is crucial to successful international expansion, which for countries with small domestic markets, such as Australia, is imperative to prosper or even survive. Hence my research has important practical implications for business in Australia.

My approach to research has been guided by three principles: conducting innovative research in new areas; designing rigorous, systematic and large-scale empirical tests of core models and theories in international management; and challenging commonly held beliefs through a critical evaluation of established work. As a result my research has consistently pushed the frontiers in the area of International Management and has become highly cited by academics in the field.

This section is divided into five sub-sections. In Sections A and B, I will show that my research programs are of major international significance and that both the quality and impact of my research and publications display exceptional distinction. In sections C and D, I will provide evidence of my international network and reputation and show that I have played a major role in mentoring junior colleagues and collaborators. Section E discusses my funding record.

1

I divide my research activities into five research programs. While the range of programs clearly shows my breadth of scholarship, all five programs are firmly located in the area of International Management. My three longest running research programs have already made very significant contributions to the field; the impact and contributions from the two newer programs will certainly increase over the next few years as their results and work in progress are published and disseminated. Taken together, they form a comprehensive portfolio of established and new work.

Program 1: International Human Resource Management and staffing policies (1992- ...)

My initial research was in the area of comparative industrial relations and International Human Resource Management (IHRM). Early publications in this area were textbook chapters and study guides; it also resulted in my first major publication, an influential research-based textbook on IHRM (Sage 1995) that I co-edited. I completed the second edition of this book (published late 2003); the new edition enlisted top scholars from a dozen different countries as contributors. Sage publications has already requested me to start working on a 3rd edition, to be published late 2008. Chapters in this book are widely cited in the academic literature. The first edition has so far drawn 94 Google Scholar (GS) citations, while the second edition has already gathered 21 GS citations in its short life.[1]

One aspect of my PhD work (of which more in program 2) focused on international staff transfer as a control mechanism in multinational companies (MNCs). This work and associated research into staffing policies has resulted in a significant number of conference and journal publications (# 9, 35-37, 41, 57-59, 67-70, 96, 113). My work was the *first to confirm empirically* that expatriates play a major role in controlling subsidiaries, both through direct supervision and, more subtly, through socialisation and the creation of informal communication networks. It also was the *first to provide detailed information* about staffing policies in a large sample of MNCs. Up till then academics had mostly relied on one much smaller scale study conducted in the 1970s. My three major refereed journal publications on this topic published in 2001 in *Employee Relations, Human Resource Management* and *Journal of World Business* have so far gathered more than 30 ISI citations and 65 GS citations. According to GS these articles were respectively the 3rd , 2nd and 1st most cited papers published in these journals in 2001.

Recently, I have shifted my attention to the role that expatriates play in knowledge transfer within MNCs. In this area, the work with a research student, Barry Hocking, has resulted in several conference papers (# 96, 113) and two articles (# 29, 48). We show that learning by expatriates is an underestimated strategic assignment outcome and that varying combinations of global and local knowledge access and communication are crucial in achieving the MNC's goals of global efficiency, national responsiveness and worldwide learning. Another student, Sebastian Reiche, has been working with me looking at the role of social capital in knowledge sharing through expatriate assignments. A revised version of his conceptual model has been presented at conferences (# 89, 110) and is currently under review at the *Journal of International Business Studies* (# 55). Work in this area combines both the individual and company level of analysis, which is highly needed, but so far quite unusual in this field.

Program 2: HQ-subsidiary relationships in MNCs (1993-...)

This research program investigates various aspects of strategy, structure, control mechanisms, and Human Resource Management in multinational companies (MNCs), and includes a large-scale international mail survey in which I collected data from 287 subsidiaries in 22 countries. This work culminated in my PhD thesis, which was subsequently published as *Managing the Multinationals* by Edward Elgar (1999) (# 1). This book has been widely cited with 30 ISI citations and 78 GS citations.

My interest in this area first led to two book chapters in my research-based IHRM textbook (see program 1) and a chapter in an edited research book (#10). My subsequent journal articles expanded on the analysis in *Managing the Multinationals* and focused on specific topics in more detail:

---

[1] Google Scholar (GS) data are used in this application in addition to, or instead of, ISI data since GS includes citations in non-ISI journals (many good International Business journals are not ISI listed), conference/working papers and to some extent citations in books. Hence it provides a fairer picture of an academic's total impact. Searches for author impact and journal impact in GS have been conducted with the Publish or Perish software that is freely available from my website (www.harzing.com/pop.htm).

2

- An article in *Journal of International Business Studies* (2000) (#39) provided the *first large-scale empirical test and extension* of what is probably the most influential typology in the field of international management – the Bartlett and Ghoshal typology of MNCs – and has been cited extensively [18 cites in ISI, 63 in GS as the 5th most cited paper published in this journal in 2000 (out of >50 papers)].
- An article in *Strategic Management Journal* (2002) (#34) broke new ground in drawing the attention to the *management* (as opposed to the widely studied initial *choice*) of different international market entry modes as being of crucial importance to the success of the MNC. As such it provided a fresh and novel approach to a widely studied area as has been cited extensively [19 cites in ISI, 48 in GS as the 14th most cited paper published in this journal in 2000 (out of >90 papers)].
- My lead article in *Organization Studies* (2003) (#32) reports on the *first large-scale empirical study* to investigate the embeddedness of MNC strategy and control mechanisms in their country of origin. It was awarded the Roland Calori prize for best article in OS in 2003-2004 and has been cited extensively [16 cites in ISI, 18 in GS as the 6th most cited paper published in this journal in 2000 (out of >60 papers)]. A second article providing a conceptual review of the country-of-origin effects was published in *Management International Review* (#30).

A survey conducted in collaboration with Prof. Niels Noorderhaven provided data for 175 subsidiaries of MNCs headquartered the US, Japan, France, Germany, UK and the Netherlands. In 2006 we published two papers from these data (# 19, 20). Analogous to my JIBS article, the first paper provided the *first large-scale empirical test and extension* of what is the most influential typology in the field of subsidiary management – the Gupta & Govindarajan typology of subsidiaries based on knowledge flows. Reflecting my current geographical location, we have also published a paper on the role of geographical distance on the management of subsidiaries, comparing Australian and New Zealand subsidiaries to subsidiaries all over the world. A third paper, currently under revision for *Journal of International Business Studies* (#54), investigates the determinants of knowledge flows in MNCs and points to the increasing role of inter-subsidiary flows in this field. A final paper (#16) in this area (an invited contribution to a Blackwell research volume *Images of the MNC* to appear in 2007) compares the impact of country-of-origin on HQ-subsidiary relationships for German, Japanese, British and US MNCs at two points in time (1995 and 2002). As such this paper provides a much-needed *large-scale empirical test* (and dismissal) of the claim that management practices in MNCs are converging to an Anglo-American model.

Program 3: The International Research process (1995 - ...)

This program consists of a number of projects that focus on research *process* issues in (international) research and often result in a *critical evaluation of received wisdom*. My first contribution in this area (#45) was to disprove the firmly entrenched myth of high expatriate failure rates that had been created by extensive (mis-) quotations and careless referencing. This paper has been cited very extensively [37 cites in ISI; 81 in GS as the 1st most cited paper (out of >50 papers) published in this journal in 1995 (by a wide margin, the next paper has only 46 cites)] and is also reprinted in the International Library of Essays on Business and Management, published by Ashgate in 2007. A subsequent large-scale update (#35) placed the myth of high expatriate failure into the wider context of the way in which referencing errors undermine our academic credibility[2], and has already been well-cited [10 cites in ISI; 22 in GS as the 13th most cited paper published in this journal in 2002 (out of >50 papers)]. A final recent article in this series with Claus Christensen (#24) suggests abandoning the concept of expatriate failure altogether.

In the area of entry mode studies, the Kogut and Singh (1988) index of cultural distance has reached an almost unassailable status. My very detailed and *critical review* of research in this area (#28) shows that there is little or no evidence for the relationship between cultural distance and entry mode choice. Even though it was only published very recently (2003/2004) with 13 GS citations it is already the 13th most cited contribution (out of > 150 papers) in the *Advances in International (Comparative) Management* series since its inception in 1984.

---

[2] Nancy Adler, Professor at McGill University (Canada) and one of the most prominent researchers in the Intl. Management field, was one of the reviewers of this article. She signed her review and mentioned that the paper had *"the potential to make an extraordinary contribution"*. In commenting on both this article and my articles dealing with the impact of language on questionnaire response (see below), Michael Bond, Professor at the Chinese University of Hong Kong and one of the most prominent researchers in Cross Cultural Psychology, called me *"the conscience of cross-cultural psychology that keeps us all honest"*.

3

Another line of research in this program concerns the process of data collection through international mail surveys. Two articles that draw lessons about international mail surveys (*International Business Review*, 1997, #42; *Industrial Marketing Management*, 2000, #39) are widely used by researchers in the field, since they are the *two only published articles* dealing with this topic. Both papers have been highly cited, with a combined total of 52 ISI citations and nearly 100 GS citations. Another article comparing response styles across countries has received great interest at conference presentations and was recently published in the *Intl Jnl of Cross cultural Management* (#22). This is the *first study* to provide a detailed analysis of response styles in a large number of countries.

An important aspect of international mail survey research is language: subjects often respond in a language that is not their own. I have initiated and led an international project that aimed to find out if language has an impact on the way that subjects respond. Apart from some old and very small-scale studies comparing just two languages there has been *no previous research* in this important area. The project involved collaborators from 26 different countries collecting data from nearly 4,500 respondents. Several conference papers have been presented about this project, and the first journal article with a preliminary analysis for seven countries was published in *Language and Intercultural Communication* (#33). A spin-off article dealing with a comparison of pre- and post-September 11 data for our US sample (#26) drew important conclusions for cross-national research. The complete results of this project were published in 2005 in *The International Journal of Cross Cultural Management* (#22) and showed that the use of English-language questionnaires may obscure national differences.

In pursuing research in this area, I have also become interested in critically assessing the impact of academic research as well as the role of editors and editorial boards in the publishing process. Recently, I have therefore started several new projects in this area. First, with Isabel Metz, I am looking at determinants of editorial board diversity (both gender and cultural). We have collected data for 60 journals, covering 10,000 editorial board members and nearly 10,000 articles. Four papers are planned from this study and the first paper is currently under revision at the *Academy of Management Journal*. Second, I have developed an interest in comparisons of research output across countries. In this context, my recent article on the publication patterns of Australian academics (High Volume, Low Impact?, #21) has generated considerable attention. It even resulted in an official thank-you memo from the Vice Chancellor. Based on this publication and my Journal Quality List (see below) I have been invited by the ANZIBA (Australian New Zealand International Business Academy) executive committee to advise them on journal rankings. The Directors of Research Network in the UK, a committee of BAM (British Academy of Management) asked me to deliver a keynote speech on the value and use of journal rankings at their annual conference. An article with John Mingers (#53) providing a statistical analysis of my journal ranking lists extends the service already provided to researchers through my Journal Quality List (see below).

Program 4: Language in International Business (2001 - ...)

One of the first barriers that companies face on the path to internationalisation is difference in language. Surprisingly, language in international business has remained a *virtually ignored research field*. Part of the reason may be researchers have been deterred by the cross-disciplinary nature of the subject. Another factor may be the pre-eminence of Anglophone researchers who have a reduced perception of the importance of language. A third factor might be the enormous influence of Hofstede. His work has dominated cultural research for the past decade and has developed into a system for measuring cultural distance thereby providing researchers with a practical, easy to use and "reliable" measure of culture.

Perhaps the most serious barrier to language research in business has been the absence of clear conceptual frameworks and operationalisations. Researchers will not be able to dissect the nature and implications of language problems until they have answers to the questions "what exactly is it about language that creates the problem", "how can it be defined" and "how can it be measured"? These questions can only be answered within the context of the socio-linguistic theory that explains how the language barrier actually works. With Alan Feely, I have therefore written various conceptual papers that deal with these issues. An early version of this work was presented at the 2002 *Academy of Management* meeting (#119) and has been accepted for Cross Cultural Management (#49), while a paper dealing with language management in MNCs was also published in *Cross Cultural Management* (2003) (#31). The latter has already gathered 10 citations in GS and is the most cited paper published in the journal that year.

4

In 2005 I have started a new project that investigates the impact of language on management practices within MNCs. This project links the work in Program 3 with this program and leads us from: *"Do respondents subconsciously adjust their responses in a way that reflects the cultural values associated with the language of the questionnaire?"* to *"Do managers adjust their management style in a way that reflects the cultural values associated with the language in which they manage".* Using a critical incident technique data have been collected with (executive) MBA students in 20 different countries. This project is now in the analysis phase. In addition, two experiments have been designed, one in the Netherlands and one in Melbourne that allow me to isolate the impact of language on decision-making. The first experiment has already been conducted and results show that language has an impact on the competitive behaviour of students: a prisoner's dilemma game played in English leads to significantly more competitive behaviour than when the same game is played in Dutch. The results are currently written up for submission to the *Academy of Management Journal*. A second and third phase of this project aims to further develop and test the language barrier model. The second phase involved nearly 50 interviews in subsidiaries and HQs in Japan and Germany, which are currently in the process of being transcribed and translated. The third phase involves a mail survey in China and Australia. I have secured an ARC Discovery Grant of $185,000 to conduct these projects.

Program 5: Transfer of HRM practices in MNCs (1998 - ...)

One of the central questions in the literature on MNCs is the extent to which their subsidiaries act and behave as local firms (local isomorphism) versus the extent to which their practices resemble those of the parent company or some global standard (internal consistency). The purpose of this program (conducted in collaboration with Barbara Myloni and Markus Pudelko) is to provide an insight into the interplay of cultural, institutional and organisational factors that affect the transfer of HRM practices across borders.

As is the case in many other areas of international management, previous research in this area has focused mostly on Japan and the USA as home/host countries. Within Europe, research has almost exclusively focused on Germany and the UK. In this program, we therefore purposefully selected an *underrepresented research setting*, Greece and focused on European MNCs rather than Japanese and American MNCs only. Data have been collected for 135 subsidiaries and local companies in Greece. Several conference papers have been presented (#90, 97, 98, 116, 125, 127), two journal article have been published (#25, 27) and one further article is in press (#50).

A new research project in collaboration with Markus Pudelko (University of Edinburgh) compares HRM models among Japanese, German and US MNCs and their subsidiaries. It is based on a unique database with primary information on 849 HQs and subsidiaries collected over the past five years by Dr. Pudelko. Our results lead to the rather surprising conclusion that for what might be considered to be the most localized of functions – human resource management – convergence to a world-wide best practices model (also called dominance effect) is clearly present for Japanese and German MNCs and as such *challenges established beliefs* in this area. Our results suggests that MNCs might limit transfer of practices to what they consider to be their core competencies and converge to best practices in other areas. The first paper resulting from this project (#47) won the best paper award in the track International Strategic Management and was nominated for the Temple AIB Best Paper Award. It has just been accepted for *Human Resource Management*, the top journal in the field of HRM.

B. QUALITY AND IMPACT OF MY RESEARCH AND PUBLICATIONS

Impact can be measured in many ways. In my research I continually attend to two goals. One goal is having an impact on the academic research community, and here impact might be best assessed by journal quality and citation counts. However another goal, and one near and dear to my research heart, is having an impact on practice and policy. Here impact might be assessed by my success in disseminating my research findings to practicing managers, where academic research has the opportunity to impact government and business practice. Publishing in local and regional journals is a key means to achieve this goal.

My publications have appeared in all major International Business Journals (*Journal of International Business Studies, Management International Review, Journal of World Business, International Business Review* and *Journal of International Management*) as well in top journals in the fields of Strategic Management (*Strategic Management Journal*), Human Resource Management (*Human Resource Management*), Organisation Studies (*Organization Studies*), Organisational Behaviour (*Journal of Organizational Behavior*), Market-

5

ing (*Industrial Marketing Management*) and Industrial Relations (*European Journal of Industrial Relations*) and a range of specialised journals in International HRM and Cross-cultural management. The fact that I have published in top journals in virtually all sub-disciplines in Management illustrates the breadth of my scholarship.

Evaluating journal quality is fraught with problems. However, there can be little argument that the journals I have published in are among the top-ranked journals in Management. I will use SSCI impact scores to illustrate this. Impact scores in Management are much lower than in the Sciences or even in Management's foundation disciplines of Economics, Sociology and Psychology. An impact score of > 1.0 is generally considered to be reflective of an absolute top-level journal, while an impact score between 0.5 and 1.0 is reflective of a very good international journal. Only 30 journals in Management have impact scores above 1.0 and only 56 have an impact score above 0.5. Using the average impact scores for 2003-2005 (latest available year), I have seven publications (published or in press) in journals with an impact score above 1.0: *Strategic Management Journal* (2.20), *Human Resource Management* (2.12, 3 times), *Journal of Organizational Behavior* (1.40), *Journal of International Business Studies* (1.31), *Organization Studies* (1.27), as well as a range of journals with impact scores above 0.5: *European Journal of Industrial Relations* (0.86) *Journal of World Business* (0.78), *Industrial Marketing Management* (0.74), *The International Journal or Human Resource Management* (0.56) (three times). It is important to note that many very good Management journals (including all regional journals) are not ISI ranked. While in the Sciences 80-90% of the academic journals are ISI ranked, this is the case for only about 30-40% of the Management journals. Journals such as *Management International Review, International Business Review*[3], and *Journal of International Management* are not ISI ranked but are generally considered to be top-5 journals in International Business. I currently have co-authored papers under revision at the *Academy of Management Journal* (2.73), *Journal of International Business Studies* (1.31). I also expect to submit at least two articles resulting from my ARC Discovery Grant project to the *Academy of Management Review* and/or the *Academy of Management Journal*.

A remarkable aspect of my early publications in top ISI-ranked journals is that - with one exception - all nine papers are single-authored, the final paper (in *Org. Studies*) being first-authored. The four recent (2004 and 2007/2008) papers in IJHRM/HRM were co-authored. While publishing single-authored articles in these journals is relatively rare to start with (e.g. only 1 in 4 articles published in JIBS since 2000 is single-authored; for Strategic Management Journal this is only 1 in 5), publishing sole authored articles in these top journals from outside North America is very unusual. For example, I am one of only two academics associated with an Australian university who has ever published a single-authored article in *Journal of International Business Studies* (JIBS) since it was established 37 years ago. The fact that I have managed to publish a single-authored article in top (US) Management journals not just once, but no less than eight times is a unique achievement in itself.

The quality of my work is also evidenced by the fact that one of my articles won the prestigious Roland Calori price for the best article in Organization Studies in 2003-2004. Jean-Claude Thoenig in his laudatio [http://www.egosnet.org/about/harzing_sorge_prize.shtml]:

> This is an OS style scientific paper at its best. It fits perfectly the three criteria listed above (rooted in Social Sciences, display methodological quality and theoretical innovativeness, highlight our understanding of differences and relatedness) and the EGOS values. It also addresses an issue that common sense had oversimplified in the past. In a way Harzing and Sorge findings about MMEs could be a lesson for science and for what EGOS aims at in its field of knowledge; to give the floor to a diversity of expressions so that they can dialogue and cross-fertilize. To avoid normal science syndromes, let us be multinational while keeping our research fertilized by our respective "countries of origin" perspectives and traditions.

An earlier reference by Srilata Zaheer for my application to Associate Professor perfectly illustrates my research approach:

> Her insights in the latter area on mail survey responses and the role of language in influencing response rates is path-breaking work that will be of lasting importance. In choosing her research questions, she challenges taken-for-granted assumptions and this makes her work particularly interesting and insightful. What is also particularly commendable in her work is that she engages in difficult primary data collection, often engaging teams of collaborators, instead of following the much easier, but less insightful path of using standard published datasets and "researching under the streetlight" that is taken by many young scholars. Her international reputation as a scholar and her ability

---

[3] Whilst International Business Review was ISI listed in 2006, the other IB journals are still unlisted.

More recently I have also started to publish some of my work in local and regional journals (e.g. *European Management Journal, Asia Pacific Journal of Management* and *Australian Journal of Management*) in order to communicate with local networks. Although this is frowned upon by some, I consider these outlets to be the most appropriate outlets for the work in question (e.g. student mobility in the European Union, Australian and New Zealand subsidiaries and the publication patterns of Australian academics). It should also be noted that a journal such as APJM has an acceptance rate of only 15% (Delios, APJM, vol 22, 115-121, 2005) and should hence be seen as a good international journal.

What I consider to be even more important than publishing in high-level journals is publishing work that has impact, both in the academic and practitioner world. As Nederhof (2006)[4] indicates the focus on the citation impact of journals rather than that of individual publications carries significant disadvantages. Therefore, whilst I have referred to journal impact factors in this case for promotion, a heavier emphasis will be put on the impact of **my publications** than on the impact of the **journal** in which they appeared. In terms of academic impact my publications have been extremely successful. At the time of writing 289 citations are listed for my work in the Social Science Citation Index. Another 50-odd ISI citations are listed for chapters in my edited IHRM book, illustrating the impact of this book on the field. In evaluating citations, one should realise that citations in many good international management journals (e.g. *Management International Review, International Business Review, Journal of International Management, Thunderbird International Business Review* and *International Journal of Cross-cultural Management*) are not listed in the SSCI. A recent special issue of TIBR on expatriation (Dec 2004) for instance included 10 citations to my work.

My work is also cited regularly in research books, conference/working papers and articles not included in the SSCI. As of January 2007, Google Books listed some 150 books that included one or more references to my work. As an example, the second edition of Geert Hofstede's *Culture's Consequences* includes seven references to my work. Google scholar (which includes citations non-ISI journals and conference/working papers), lists more than 650 citations for Harzing (there are no other academics with my last name). Since much of my published work is recent, I expect the number of citations to grow rapidly. My number of SSCI citations has increased by 99 in the last year alone. It is important to note that with a handful of exceptions all citations are to single-authored work (in most cases) or first-authored work (in two cases). Most of my co-authored work is recent and hence has not yet had the time to gather citations. This means that my citation record is based on my *individual* work and is not inflated by (networks of) co-authors. In addition, the reach of my work is truly international. While 30% of my citations come from authors based in the USA, 20%/15% each come from authors in the UK and China (Hong Kong), 10% each from authors in Australia and the Netherlands and 5% each from authors in Canada and Germany.

In order to put my research impact into perspective I have provided a comparison below with three groups of scholars: academics who have been promoted to professor in our Faculty in 2005/2006 (4 academics), established IB professors at UQ, Sydney and AGSM (4 academics), academics who are or recently were established professors in the Department of Management and Marketing (5 academics). Comparison is based on a number of accepted bibliometric indicators, including the recently introduced h-index[5] that has become a widely accepted "summary statistic" that combines both quantity and quality. The h index is seen to have the advantage that it gives a robust estimate of the broad impact of a scientist's cumulative research contributions. This means that the h index is insensitive to a set of lowly cited (non cited) papers or to one or several highly cited papers: A scientist with very few highly cited papers (a 'one-hit wonder') or, alternatively, many lowly cited papers will have a weak h index, whilst scientists with a steady stream of well-cited papers will have a strong h-index. The h-index was calculated using Google Scholar data. As explained earlier Google Scholar data are more comprehensive than ISI data. For comparative purposes the number of *articles* citing the academic's work in ISI journals in 2006 is also listed as a measure of contemporary influence. Please note that this figure is different from the number of *citations* as one article can (and in my cases usually does) contain multiple citations to an academic's work.

---

[4] A.J. Nederhof (2006) Bibliometric monitoring of research performance in the Social Sciences and Humanities: A review, Scientometrics, vol. 66/1, 81-100.
[5] An academic has index h if h of his/her Np papers have at least h citations each, and the other (Np-h) papers have no more than h citations each. Hence an academic with a h-index of 13 has 13 papers with **at least** 13 citation each.

Table 1: Bibliometric comparison with other professors, mean and range are given for each indicator.
[Please note that the Google Scholar data this table is no longer representative because of a substantial increase in GS coverage]

Group	h-index	1st authored papers in h-index	Single-authored papers in h-index	Number of ISI citing articles (2006 only)	Number of years as professor
2005/2006 promotions	Mean: 6.3 Range: 4-8	Mean: 4.3 Range: 3-5	Mean: 3.0 Range: 2-4	Mean: 15 Range: 3-34	Recently appointed
IB professors at top Oz unis	Mean: 9.0 Range: 4-16	Mean: 3.3 Range: 1-6	Mean: 1.5 Range: 0-3	Mean: 10 Range: 3-21	15 years (4-28 years)
DoMM established professors	Mean: 14.0 Range: 6-22	Mean: 5.0 Range: 0-11	Mean: 2.0 Range: 0-4	Mean: 46 Range: 8-102	14 years (10-19 years)
Anne-Wil Harzing	13	13	10	63	N/A

From the above comparison, it is clear that my overall academic impact exceeds that of all recently promoted professors and all IB professors at top universities in Australia, even though the latter have on average been in post for 15 years. It also compares well with established professors in the Department of Management and Marketing that have been promoted to a professorial level 10-19 years ago. What is particularly remarkable is my very high number of highly cited 1st authored and single-authored papers in comparison to other professors. This means that my citation record is based on my *individual* work and that there is no possibility of it being inflated by (networks of) famous co-authors.

Although my research output is primarily aimed at academics, I have always been interested in sharing the results of academic work with practitioners. In the mid-1990s I was Secretary of the "Research vs. Practice" committee of the NVP (Dutch Association for Personnel Management) and wrote a monthly column ("From the Ivory Tower") in the practitioner journal *Personeelsbeleid* (Personnel Management). The results of my PhD thesis were written up in several business reports and I wrote more detailed reports for a number of the companies involved. More recently, my work has been reviewed at websites of consultancy firms and semi-governmental organisations (e.g. expatica.com on determining success in expatriation; Primacy Relocation on "Are you globally assigning bees, spiders or bears"; CILT (National Centre for Languages) on language in international business surveys). In June 2004, the European Publisher Business Digest featured a dossier based on my articles on language management with a commentary of a former IBM USA vice-president. It also discussed one of my other articles on country-of-origin effects on MNC strategy and structure. In recent years I have started using my publications about expatriate management, MNC typologies and language management in MNCs in my classes. Assessment for these classes requires students to apply the theories to their current or previous work experience and I have been pleasantly surprised at the ease with which students are able to apply my work in a business setting. In 2004 I assisted the Melbourne Newcomers Network with the development of a survey to assess the needs of newcomers. My presentation of the results of the survey and most notably the fact that newcomers (both international and interstate newcomers) feel a newcomer in Australia longer and find it more difficult to make friends than in any other country have generated a lot of attention.

C. Significant Role in Research Projects and International Reputation

Although I conduct the core of my research work individually, I have also assumed major responsibilities in research supervision and mentoring (see sub-section D), and have recently **initiated, designed and led** three large-scale international research projects.

The first project dealt with the interaction between language and culture (see program 3), and involved over 30 research collaborators in 26 countries. I created the research design for the project, constructed the questionnaire with its supporting materials, and supervised the translation process for all (more than twenty) languages involved. I also recruited and managed the research collaborators through a 2-year process of data collection and consolidation. Because several collaborators in this project were PhD students or junior academics, I also fulfilled a mentoring role for many of them.

The second project dealt with headquarters-subsidiary relationships (see research programs 1, 2 and 4), and replicated and extended the work done for my PhD. This project was conducted in collaboration with Prof. Niels Noorderhaven (Tilburg University, The Netherlands); my responsibilities were the research and ques-

8

tionnaire design, and the co-ordination of the data collection process. The data analysis and publication process responsibilities are shared equally.

The third project extends the work done in the first project and involves more than 20 countries. I created the research design for the project, constructed the questionnaire, and arranged for translation and pilot testing for all of the languages involved. This involved interaction with nearly 100 casual RAs. I also recruited research collaborators in all countries. The fact that I was able to enlist the help of more than 20 collaborators in less than a week indicates that academics are very keen to collaborate with me.

My international reputation and international network of contacts are well established through consistently publishing in high level international journals and active participation in the international academic community. As my research programs show, I have made a significant impact in the field through **novel, critical and groundbreaking** contributions. Even though a lot of my published work is recent, the very large number of citations to it demonstrates that it has already significantly influenced the work of other researchers in the field. A related aspect that confirms my international reputation is the number of journals for which I have been asked to review. Over the past ten years I have reviewed manuscripts for well over fifteen different journals (see *Service to the Discipline* for further details).

As a result of my publication record and extensive reviewing experience, I have been appointed as departmental editor Culture & Cognition for *Journal of International Business Studies*, associate editor Strategy for the *Australian Journal of Management* as well as associate editor for *The International Journal of Cross Cultural Management* and consulting editor for the *International Journal of Management Reviews*. I am also on the editorial board of *International Business Review* (a European IB journal), *European Management Review* (the journal of the European Academy of Management) and *Human Resource Management* (the top journal in the field of HRM) and the newly establish *European Journal of International Management*.

My international reputation is also clearly evidenced by the ease with which I can interest people in participating in my research projects and in committee work for the Academy of Management (see the *Service to the Academic Community* section, later on). In the past 5 years I have secured collaboration from more than 75 academics from nearly 50 different countries in various research projects, and have recruited nearly fifty country representatives in my role as Chair of the Membership Involvement Committee of the International Management Division of the Academy of Management. Many of the collaborators volunteer their services because of my reputation in the field. As a further indication of my standing in the field, I am particularly proud that many well-known and highly regarded academics[6] in the area of International and Comparative HRM and Industrial Relations readily consented to write a chapter for the 2nd edition of my edited research-based textbook on IHRM[7].

More recently, I am receiving an increasing number of invitations to contribute to books and journals. I was asked to contribute a chapter to *"Images of the Multinational Firm"*, in the Blackwell series of "Images of...." which take a critical look at a specific management field. This book is edited by two highly respected academics of Warwick Business School (Glenn Morgan & Simon Collinson). Other contributors to the book (Alan Rugman, Eleanor Westney, John Cantwell, Richard Whitley, Christel Lane and Paul Edwards) are all full professors at very prestigious universities and have very long-standing reputations in their field. I was also asked to contribute a key-note paper on International HRM to the second annual www.dialogin.com e-conference organised by The Delta Intercultural Academy and provided the key-note speech at the 4th workshop on International Strategy and Cross Cultural Management in 2006. I have served as an expert in a Delphi study on the *'Futures of Teaching and Learning International Business*, conducted by Victoria Univ. of Wellington and Turku School of Economics and Business Administration and was nominated by multiple consortium members based on my contributions to the field of international business. *Journal of Management Inquiry* asked me to write a commentary on one of their articles, while *Asia Pacific Journal of Management* asked me to write one of their "Perspectives" papers for 2006. I was invited by Edward Elgar to edit a Handbook of IHRM and was also invited to contribute a section on cross-cultural management to the International Encyclopedia of Organization Studies, edited by Stewart Clegg & James Bailey. Unfortunately, I had to de-

---

[6] For example, Prof Paul Evans (INSEAD), Prof. Vladimir Pucik (IMD), Prof. Terry Jackson (EAP Oxford), Prof. Malcolm Warner (Cambridge), Prof. Richard Hyman (LSE), Profs. Keith Sisson and Paul Marginson (both Warwick).
[7] I also managed to get all of them not only to complete their chapters on time, but to do so in a very collaborative spirit, as is illustrated by the following comment by Keith Sisson: *"Many thanks for your comments – supreme efficiency as ever. I think every one is well taken and I will make sure the final version incorporates them."*

9

cline these four requests, as I decided that my already high workload would not allow me to do full justice to them.

Although I have received many invitations for visiting Professorships, I have been unable to accept any of these, as I have not had the fortune to qualify for sabbatical leave until 2004. In 2004, I decided it was more important for me to embed myself in the Australian academic community and spent my sabbatical visiting universities in Australia. I was recently asked (and have accepted) an appointment as occasional Visiting Professor at the University of Strathclyde (UK), a major centre for IB research in the UK.

D. RESEARCH SUPERVISION AND MENTORING OF JUNIOR COLLEAGUES

Research supervision has always been an integral and important part of my work. In my previous positions at the Universities of Tilburg, Maastricht and Bradford, I have supervised some 25 MA dissertations, mostly in the area of international management and (international) HRM. Since my appointment at the University of Melbourne, I have supervised two PhD students and two Masters by Research student to completion, and am currently the primary supervisor of two further PhD students. In addition, I regularly receive visiting PhD students or postdoctoral students from other countries, who express a strong desire to work with me. In 2007, three students from Austria and Germany will visit me for periods of 1 to 6 months.

I am actively trying to build up a group of research students in the area of international (human resource) management and cross-cultural management. My approach to research supervision is to ensure that my students develop themselves as well-rounded academics rather than simply finishing their theses. After the initial phase, I treat them as junior colleagues, not students. I value academic discourse highly and I actively encourage them to join professional associations as early in their studies as possible, to go to Summer schools and conferences, and to build up their own networks.

In addition, I try to support academic colleagues, research collaborators and students both within and outside my university wherever possible. Ever since my academic web site went online in 1999, an increasing number of PhD students and young colleagues from other universities contact me to discuss their ideas or ask me to evaluate their papers. Even though this takes up a lot of my time, I feel it is part of creating a supportive academic community for young researchers. Over the past six years I have helped dozens of colleagues, collaborators and research students with suggestions, tips, writing and journal submission advice. Some representative testimonials:

I became acquainted with Prof. Harzing in 2002 upon completion of my PhD degree. At the time I had contacted her with a request to review my thesis, to which she agreed without hesitation. Since then, Prof. Harzing has been a primary mentor and source of invaluable advice. I have spent many years in Eastern Europe, where access to resources is lacking and opportunities are scarce, especially for young academics. Prof. Harzing invited me to join her International Language & Culture project and later as a representative for Lithuania in the Membership Involvement Committee of the IM division of the Academy of Management, of which she was chair at the time. These opportunities were key in motivating me to continue as an academic, as they provided not only valuable research experience but also networking opportunities, and were also instrumental in helping me to obtain much needed funding for my own research projects and attendance at conferences. Because of my involvement in the IMD, I was able to attend the Academy of Management annual meeting in 2005, as a participant in a Junior Faculty Consortium and the only (and likely first) attendee from Lithuania, and thus secure funding from my own university, where funds are virtually non-existent. I have had the opportunity to participate in other international research projects since the Language & Culture project, and in none of the others was collaboration and communication among researchers as close or implementation as organized. Most importantly and most recently, Prof. Harzing served as one of my main references for a recent employment search. I am quite certain that my involvement in her research projects, as well as the advice she provided and the insight I obtained from working with her, were among the main reasons that I received an employment offer. Had I not been given the above opportunities, I would likely not have the motivation that I do now. I know that many other young academics have also benefited from her guidance. [Audra Mockaites, University of Vilnius, from Feb. 2006 Victoria University of Wellington, audra-@mockaitis.com, solicited feedback.]

Finally, I want to thank Dr. Anne-Wil Harzing for her encouragement and leading by example. One cannot hope for better guidance in terms of good scholarship, professional assertiveness and personal humbleness [Thomas Hippler, thomas.hippler@gmx.de, a German PhD student doing his PhD in Ireland, whom I have supported throughout his candidature, written in the acknowledgements of his PhD, reproduced with his permission]. He also wrote in his letter to me: "The confidence to pursue such a course (a non-traditional PhD) of work partly stemmed from reading

10

your article about the myth of high expatriate failure rates. It showed that you can indeed write against beliefs widely held in your field if you believe them to be incorrect and can produce the evidence to back up your claim".

I have known Anne-Wil Harzing since I joined the University of Melbourne in July 2003 as Lecturer in Strategy International Business. From my very first days with the Department Anne-Wil has been a supportive colleague, showing genuine interest in my professional development. A few months later I approached Anne-Wil with the request to become my mentor, which she accepted without hesitation. I was impressed by Anne-Wil's research experience, publication record and, more generally, her professionalism in all aspects of academic life. I could see that she was highly regarded by our colleagues and I had little doubt that she would be an effective mentor and a worthy role model. In her mentoring role, Anne-Wil has always been willing to discuss my research ideas and teaching challenges, provided useful advice regarding journal publications and grant applications, and invested a lot of her time in giving feedback on my articles. For example, Anne-Wil assisted me in preparing two faculty grants applications (both were successful) On her advice I joined the Early Career Researcher program in 2004-2005, which is helping me to advance my research career. I will never forget the advice Anne-Wil gave me on how to select PhD students, which I have followed closely. In general, Anne-Wil has been a source of inspiration and moral support throughout my 2.5 years with the University, and I hope that this mentoring relationship will continue. [Tatiana Zalan, tzalan@unimelb.edu.au, solicited feedback.]

E. FUNDING

Until recently my funding record was modest, because the four universities that I worked for before joining the University of Melbourne did not have an internal grant system. And since I was still working on my PhD I could not apply for competitive government funding until 1998/1999. I took the first available opportunity to do so in the UK with a submission to the ESRC (equivalent to the ARC), but although my proposal was among the 26% alpha-rated proposals, I was not successful (only 2 of the 11 alpha-rated proposals, i.e. less than 5% of the total proposals were funded). Since by that time I had decided I wanted to leave the UK, I had to postpone further attempts at securing research funding.

In Melbourne, I have taken every available opportunity to apply for research funding. I have secured a University Early Career Grant (2001) of $22,000 (one of only four proposals out of fourteen that was funded), and two competitive Faculty Research grants (2002 & 2004) of $10,000 and $8,000. In 2004 I was also awarded $185,000 in ARC Discovery Grant funding for a 3-year research project, where I am the only Chief Investigator. This project deals with the impact of language on management practices within MNCs (for more detail see future research plans in Part C). This was the largest ARC discovery grant awarded to a sole Chief Investigator for a project in the subject area of Management since 2002 (no data available before that time). I received 98% of the funding I requested, which is unique as the normal average funding level lies around 70% and for management projects is usually even lower. I also received funding for a 50% relief of duties, which is hardly ever awarded.

LEADERSHIP IN TEACHING

Leadership in teaching is more than being a good teacher, although that is very important. For me, leadership in teaching means more than what happens in the classroom. So much of teaching work goes on "behind the scenes" and one of my goals has been to get that "behind the scenes" material into outlets where they can be accessed by developing teachers. So I have been actively involved in writing textbook chapters and editing a textbook; as well as writing articles that might benefit (PhD) students. I have also consciously sought to continue to improve and develop my teaching.

I consider myself a very committed, experienced and effective teacher. I am passionate about my research field and my teaching has always been aimed at making students share that passion. It is never limited to transferring only textbook knowledge, and all my subjects include recent readings from academic journals. The remainder of this section includes information about the scope and impact of my teaching and my contribution to creation of teaching materials.

A. SCOPE OF TEACHING ACTIVITIES

Before joining the University of Melbourne, I had taught and co-ordinated a dozen different subjects at university level since 1991. I had also given guest lectures for EAP Oxford, Teikyo University (The Netherlands) and the Center of European Studies (The Netherlands). My prior teaching experience included a wide range of delivery methods:

- Distance learning (Open University)

11

- Problem based learning in groups of 10-15 students (Tilburg University, Maastricht University)
- Lectures, seminars and tutorials (University of Bradford, University of Melbourne)

In order to familiarise myself with the teaching environment in Melbourne, I attended several seminars at CHSE and met up personally with student support staff (e.g. Faculty Teaching & Learning Centre, Student Union, Student Counseling, Central Teaching and Learning unit). Although the surprised faces I met at these services indicated that this is apparently not common practice, I found it very helpful both as a general orientation and to establish a good rapport with other staff.

Because of the multi-faceted and integrative nature of the subjects that I teach, all of my current modules have been designated as coursework-only modules. The coursework is not of the one-size-fits-all type, but is explicitly aimed at letting students develop their own capabilities. My teaching is supported by up-to-date technological aids, including PowerPoint slides, videos, and traditional and computer-based simulations. My newly developed subject for the Masters in International Business (*Managing Across Borders*) includes an even wider range of teaching methods, and includes a guided "culture visit" that allows students to apply their theoretical knowledge in practice. Many students have told me that they dreaded this assignment, but have learned an enormous amount from it.

Table 2 lists the subjects I have taught since joining the University of Melbourne. Although only *Managing Across Borders* and the two PhD subjects were completely new, I also had to redevelop most of the other subjects, because the existing teaching materials were either unavailable or outdated. Furthermore, as I only repeated one of the four subjects from my first year (mid 2001-mid 2002) at Melbourne in subsequent years, my contribution to teaching and subject development has been substantial.

Table 2: Summary of subjects taught since joining the University of Melbourne

Year	Subject	Level	# students	Role	Newly developed?	Research area?
2001	International Business Strategy (S2)	MIB	45	½ coord., ½ lectures	Yes	Partly
2001	Global Management Issues (S2)	MIB	28	½ coord., ½ lectures	Partly	Partly
2001	Strategic Management of Org. (S2)	GradDip	40	Full coord., all lectures	Yes	No
2002	Strategy (S1)	UG	320	Full coord., ½ lectures	Yes	No
2002	Global Management Issues (S2)	MIB	29	Full coord., ¾ lectures	Partly	Partly
2002	Managing Across Borders (S2)	MIB	74	Full coord., all lectures	Yes	Yes
2003	Global Management Issues (S1)	MIB	35	Full coord., all lectures	Partly	Partly
2003	Global Management Issues (S2)	MIB	35-40	Full coord., all lectures	Partly	Partly
2003	Managing Across Borders (S2)	MIB	70-80	Full coord., all lectures	Yes	Yes
2004	Global Management Issues (S1)	MIB	41	Full coord., all lectures	Partly	Partly
2005/6	Research Decisions (S1)	PhD	10 (25)*	Full coord., some lectures	Yes	Yes
2005/6	Research Methods (S1+S2)	PhD	11 (25)*	Full coord., some lectures	Yes	Yes

* Although only 10/11 first year students were registered for these subjects, many older year students attended and hence attendance in the sessions varied from 15 to 30

B. EVIDENCE OF IMPACT AS A TEACHER

I actively seek feedback from students to further improve my teaching and to verify whether students have mastered the concepts discussed in the lectures. In 1999 I introduced exit visas for this purpose, on which students can write (anonymously if they wish) comments and questions about the lecture. The visas allow me to adapt the content and style of teaching during the semester, if necessary.

Although not all the universities that I worked for in the Netherlands systematically conducted teaching evaluations, those evaluations that I did receive were 8 (out of 10) or better. At the University of Bradford, all of my teaching was evaluated as excellent (defined as 3.8 or more on a scale from 1 to 5) with overall scores above 4 even for UG modules, and going up to 4.7 for small postgraduate modules. My teaching evaluations at the University of Melbourne for 2001-2004 are reproduced in Table 3. I have not included the evaluations for the PhD coursework as this was taught by over 20 members of staff and hence the results are not necessarily reflective of my own teaching. Some specific feedback on my own performance in these subjects is included below.

My teaching evaluations are good and at or above the Departmental and Faculty average. I was awarded a Dean's Certificate for Excellence in Teaching for 2005. For the UG subject Strategy I spent a lot of time redesigning the subject completely, producing a very extensive course outline and a 50 page tutorial manual. I also introduced the use of Webraft as a teaching support mechanism. This was very successful and was highly

12

used with an average of 2,500 server requests a week. Comments about my share of the lecturing on the QoT forms for Strategy were highly positive.

Table 3: Summary of teaching evaluations at the University of Melbourne 2001-2004

Question	Global Mgt Issues (01-04) MIB	Managing Across Borders 02-03 MIB	International Business Strat-egy MIB	Strategic Mgmt of Org. (Grad Dip)	Strategy UG*
I had a clear idea what was expected of me	4.1	3.9	4.0	3.8	3.6
This subject was well taught	4.1	4.2	4.0	3.8	3.6
This subject was intellectually stimulating	3.8	4.0	3.9	3.8	3.5
I received helpful feedback on how I was going	4.1	3.8	3.6	3.8	2.6
Interest in the academic needs of the students	4.2	4.1	4.0	4.0	3.4

* The quantitative teaching evaluations for Strategy were not differentiated by lecturer (I took only half of the lectures), nor were tutors evaluated separately. Hence the QoT scores do not necessarily reflect the quality of my own teaching.

My QoT results for postgraduate teaching are generally good and for the Masters in International Business compare favourably with the average teaching scores for this degree. These evaluations are particularly pleasing since I insist on academically rigorous work and am not a lenient marker. Two typical quotes from QoT forms are included. Other quotes are available upon request.

> *The most interesting subject in the MIB for me. Anne-Wil showed great knowledge in this field and transferred it to us in an entertaining way. I also enjoyed the unusual assignment of the culture visit. I learned a lot!*

> *Anne-Wil is very well organised, clear, articulate and clearly an expert in her field. This subject has fitted well with others in the MIB program and also helped non-Australian students integrate with each other and local students. Classes are participative and good range of teaching styles/materials are used.*

After early student concerns about my high marking standards, I have started to make my expectations in terms of rigorous academic work even clearer at the start of semester and also provide standard feedback sheets, on which students are marked on ten specific criteria and receive extensive additional written suggestions for improvement. The response to this initiative has been extremely positive. Many students have substantially improved their essay writing skills and now receive much higher marks, even though my marking standards are unchanged. Focused feedback seems to have created a strong desire to do well for my subjects, illustrated by comments such as: *"I'll try to do better in the next assignment. I won't let you down!"* and *"I am so encouraged by my high mark, since I know you have very high standards."*

In 2005, the Department of Management introduced two PhD coursework modules into the PhD program. As director of the PhD program, I was given the responsibility to coordinate both modules. As there are more than 20 academics teaching into the coursework, coordinating it is a very significant administrative task. However, there is general agreement in the department that the introduction of the coursework has significantly improved the quality and consistency of our students' work. Despite some teething problems, student feedback was generally highly positive and the modules seem to have benefited students from all year groups. Some representative student comments in the QOT:

> *Congratulations on doing a great job and raising the standard of the PhD course. I wish I had the benefit of some courses as "refreshers" early in my PhD studies and I wouldn't be on extensions now.*

> *Thank you for an unforgettable period of stimulation, enrichment and exposure to some incredible academic role models. These courses have been the highlight of my candidature at Melbourne University.*

This comment was specifically directed to my own classes:

> *Thank you very much for letting me sit in your PhD classes. Thanks for the sincerity and passion you put in your class, especially for giving us such great advices on what to expect in the 3-year PhD life. This has been great and I feel really lucky to have the opportunity to sit with your PhD students in these classes [Dianna Li, PhD student at MBS, unsolicited feedback reproduced with her permission.].*

C. CREATION OF TEACHING MATERIALS

In addition to the (re-)developed materials for the subjects I have taught so far at the University (see subsection A, *Scope of Teaching Activities*, above) I have published seven textbook chapters and study guides, mostly in the area of Comparative Industrial Relations and International HRM (see CV).

Furthermore, I am co-editor of an influential research-based textbook on International HRM, for which I also wrote three chapters. The first edition of this book appeared in 1995 and has sold nearly 10,000 copies; the 2nd edition appeared late 2003 and is published again by Sage Publishers. With this edition, I assumed sole responsibility for finding new authors and for the bulk of the revision and editorial processes. The sales for

13

the 2nd edition have substantially exceeded those of the first edition in the first two years and it has been adopted by leading universities (e.g. London School of Economics, University of Warwick, UK; Vienna University, Austria; Uppsala University, Sweden; Essec, France). Sage publications has already requested me to start working on a 3rd edition, to be published late 2008.

My journal article on academic referencing (#35) is used in PhD programs at Tilburg University, Erasmus University, University of Texas at El Paso, University of St. Gallen, James Cook University, the University of Auckland, the University of Arizona, Stockholm School of Economics, and the University of Newcastle and is included as one of the links on Useful links for teaching faculty by Emerald Publishing. Many of my other journal articles are used as course reading in international management, cross-cultural management and international human resource management.

LEADERSHIP IN UNIVERSITY MANAGEMENT

There are so many opportunities for leadership in University management that it is difficult to know where to channel ones efforts. I found that one of the best places for me to show leadership was in a place that would capitalise on my research skills and my passion for mentoring, so I've taken on a large-scale Departmental role – the directorship of the PhD program. In addition, I have engaged in a large number of committee roles and duties. This section discusses my involvement in leadership development (section A), my various leadership/management duties (section B) and my service to the university and discipline through the development and maintenance of a major resource centre in international and cross-cultural management (section C).

A. LEADERSHIP DEVELOPMENT

Over the course of 2004, I have followed a very intensive professional development program called "Headstart". This program is designed for senior level academics expected to take on leadership roles in the near future. It consisted of a very intensive suite of some ten half and full-day courses on various aspects of management and leadership (e.g. managing change, managing difficult conversations), as well as attendance at Academic Board and various other University committees. The program also included a four-day shadowing component, in which participants shadow a Head of Department. Finally, participants conducted a Leadership Project in small groups. These projects were designed to enable participants to extend their self-knowledge and capability as leaders, to promote an understanding of leadership roles, and to stimulate thought about the broader University and external environment. Projects were real tasks, involving genuine dilemmas facing the University. My group's project was academic misconduct (e.g. exam misconduct, plagiarism) and our brief was to gather information across the twelve faculties and come up with guidelines to deal with academic misconduct in a systematic way.

I found this professional development program to be highly stimulating and beneficial. It has enabled me to develop a much better insight into the strategy and structure of the University. The interactions with senior academics from other departments were also particularly useful. I have found the Headstart course to be of tremendous value in developing my leadership potential.

B. LEADERSHIP/MANAGEMENT DUTIES AT DIFFERENT LEVELS

Currently, my most significant administrative task in the department is the directorship of the PhD program. At the moment we have about 75 students enrolled in our PhD program. I am responsible for selection of candidates and am Chair of both the Confirmation (defense of research proposal at the end of the first year) and Examination Committee. I am also coordinator of the PhD coursework modules. In my role as PhD director I have introduced the following significant changes to improve the program:

1. I tightened up the confirmation requirements, a process that was started by the previous PhD director. I have introduced written comments on the Confirmation Report in the form of memos ranging from 2 to 5 single-spaced pages. Students are normally requested to submit a revised confirmation report before they are confirmed.
2. I provide significant academic support to students on a regular basis by circulating information on conferences, journals, academic positions, useful websites, etc.
3. I introduced two PhD coursework modules, a process that was started by the previous PhD director. These modules were first offered in 2005 and there is general agreement in the department that they have significantly improved the quality and consistency of our students' work.

14

4. I have led a major review of the Department's PhD programme in 2006. In consultation with our Research and Graduate Studies Committee, I produced a report with many recommendations for improvement in the areas of admission, supervision and provision of resources. I have already implemented most of these recommendations. A significant improvement is that for the first time since inception of the programme, PhD students now receive substantial resources for conference attendance and fieldwork.

In my role as PhD director I also organised the daylong 2005 ANZIBA doctoral colloquium in which 12 students from all over Australia as well as four international students participated. Both formal and informal feedback on my work as PhD director has been overwhelmingly positive. Below I reproduce two testimonials from current PhD students.

Both in my personal name and on behalf of many of the students who attended the coursework, I would like to thank you for your involvement and dedication to the PhD program. The coursework is a real improvement to the quality and the international standing of the program, and we realise that it requires a substantial amount of work. The personal example that you have set in attending almost all of the coursework sessions, in providing comprehensive and detailed feedback on confirmation reports and presentations, and in continuously looking for improvements to the program, both in the interactions with the representatives, and with the students in general, is widely appreciated. Personally, your involvement was a strong motivation to attempt to produce both a report and a presentation of high quality. [Eric Quintane, 2nd year PhD student & PhD student rep, unsolicited feedback reproduced with his permission, e.quintane@pgrad.unimelb.edu.au]

In her first year in this position, Anne-Wil has been an outstanding PhD director. Students have genuinely appreciated, and regularly commended her on the energy and dedication with which she has embraced her role. This year has seen an extraordinary shift in both the quality and rigour of the Department's doctoral program. Students are now more appreciative of the Confirmation process as a method of quality control and risk management. Anne-Wil's rigour and scrutiny, along with her developmental feedback, gives candidates, and their supervisors, added assurance that their research proposals are likely to yield high quality, publishable findings of international standard. Anne-Wil has also devoted herself to the strategic development of the Department's PhD. program. She has worked tirelessly with the PhD representatives to identify and effectively advocate for improved student conditions, including the introduction of student home pages and an Internet forum. She strongly supported the continuation of the PhD Retreat, and secured funding to assist an unusually large contingent of students to present their work at overseas conferences. Despite her heavy workload, Anne-Wil has always been readily available as a mentor to students, and has been generous with both her time and knowledge. She has been an excellent role model for other staff, in her support for doctoral students, and through her regular sharing of information about conferences, useful web sites and specific interest groups. Her actions have fostered an atmosphere that has promoted greater student collegiality, in the form of increased information exchange, mutual support and collaborative publications. Under Anne-Wil's leadership, the profile, content and tone of the PhD program have been lifted, and along with it, the morale, competence and confidence of the student cohort. Anne-Wil provides an inspirational role model, particularly to aspiring female academics, by demonstrating that it is possible to achieve excellence in all facets of academic life. To me, Anne-Wil stands out as one of those rare academics who embodies all that is admirable, inspiring and engaging about university life: a truly memorable mentor whose challenging, formative influence will continue on with me throughout my career. [Christina Scott-Young <cscotty@unimelb.edu.au>, final year student & PhD student rep, solicited feedback reproduced with her permission]

I have also volunteered to take part in a large number of departmental and faculty level committees and University-wide initiatives.

Department

- Member of the Research and Graduate Studies Committee (RAGS), *February 2005-current*
- Chair of the Psychology Liaison Group, *February 2005-current*
- Co-editor working paper series, Australian Centre for International Business, *March 2003-current.*
- Member of the two-person Departmental Grievance committee, *2003.*
- Member of the Departmental IT Advisory group, *June 2002-June 2004.*
- Member of the Departmental Executive Committee, *January-December 2002, January-June 2004.*
- Member of a Departmental Task Force on Workload policies.
- Member of four selection committees.

Faculty

- Mentor for UG students, *May 2002-June 2004.*
- Member of the Faculty International Committee, *Jan. 2002-March 2003* (committee was discontinued).
- Member of the Faculty IT Committee, *October 2001-August 2002.*

15

University

- Member of Language Advisory Group, *February 2005-September 2006*
- Member of the Intercultural Working Party (University of Melbourne), *May 2001-May 2002.*
- Initiator and chair of the Cross-Cultural Interest Group (University of Melbourne), a group of some 15 academics/support staff from the Faculties of Economics and Commerce, Education, Arts and Medicine, covering 9 different academic departments.
- Member of the Advisory Committee for the School of International Communication and Languages (Melbourne University Private), *March 2003-September 2005.*

In addition to the formal memberships and activities, I take a strong interest in the social functioning of the department. I was the initiator and organiser of a monthly women's lunch and always attended the social gatherings for the program I was most heavily involved with (Masters in International Business). I have also been involved in the organisation of the 2002 Christmas function and organised several welcome dinners for new members of staff at my home.

C. WWW.HARZING.COM: A RESOURCE CENTRE IN INTERNATIONAL MANAGEMENT

My academic web site (www.harzing.com) provides a further service to the University and the academic community as a whole by providing a highly visible resource centre maintained by a respected scholar affiliated with the University. www.harzing.com started in 1999 as a resource site for my students in Bradford. It has since grown into a major resource site for students and academics all over the world. In addition to information about my research, publications and teaching, this web site contains information for international students and resources in international and cross-cultural management. These resources include:

- *Publish or Perish,* a software program that retrieves and analyzes academic citations is the latest addition to my site and a highly successful one. In the 3.5 months since its introduction the Publish or Perish page received more than 4,000 visitors, most of who downloaded the programme. It was mentioned twice in the Vice Chancellor's email, was listed on the Departmental Homepage and was the 3 December "Site of the Day" on HedWeb.
- *On-line papers.* Electronic versions of most of my papers. There are currently nearly 30 downloadable papers on my web site with more than 20,000 downloads in total, varying from 300 downloads for papers that have only recently been listed to more than 2,500 for one of the most popular papers.
- *Journal Quality List (JQL).* Ranking of academic journals in the field of business and management. This is the most popular page on the site, registering some 20,000 visitors in the last year alone. Academics from universities all over the world have downloaded the JQL. It is well respected as one of the major sources of journal rankings. The editor of Marketing Science, a top journal in marketing, cites it as support for his journal's high standing in his editorial (vol. 21, no 1). It was featured in BusinessWeek Online in an article on using academic journals. The JQL was also cited no less than 14 times in ISI listed journals. I get many thank-you emails, such as:
    Thanks very much for your super Journal Quality List. This really is a fantastic piece of work and I am at a loss to know how you can put in the time and what must be immense effort to keep adding, updating and improving.
  Jean Bartunek, a former president of the Academy of Management, sent me this thank-you email:
    I'm on the promotion and tenure committee at Boston College this year and was looking for rankings of journals, especially for people outside my department – and I came across your listing, which is absolutely fabulous. I just want to thank you for doing this work, which is a great help to the profession.
- *Literature database.* My personal database containing nearly six thousand literature references in the area of International Management/Business, Comparative and Cross-cultural Management. This database has been downloaded by more than 1,000 academics from all over the world. Many students and academics have contacted me to tell me how useful they find the database. Recently, it was also cited alongside ABI-INFORM, PsychInfo and SSCI as the source of a literature review (*Journal of Cross-cultural psychology,* Sept. 2005, p. 597).
- Annotated web links in the areas of Cross-Cultural Management and International Business and Expatriate Management, to sites with company and industry information, professional and international organisations, academic journals and magazines, and to all major publishers.
- Living and working in Melbourne page. This page was created to support recruitment of academic staff into the Department of Management. It contains very detailed information about living in Melbourne as well as some 30 pictures. It was used in all our recruiting efforts; other departments and many conference

16

organisers also seem to use it as a reference for information about Melbourne. In January 2007, this page drew well over 1,000 unique visitors.

The popularity of www.harzing.com is shown by the large number of page visits, which currently are in order of 15,000-20,000 per month, with visitors coming from more than 50 countries. There are dozens of web sites that include a link to the site, including those of the two most important professional associations in my field: the *Academy of International Business* and the *Academy of Management*. In its eight-year history www.harzing.com has established itself as a high-quality site which is reflected in very high Google page ranks on topics related to my research. For example Google searches for *International Management Research* and *Cross Cultural Management Research* both list www.harzing.com as their first-ranked page.

SERVICE TO THE DISCIPLINE

I am actively involved in my academic discipline and have a strong international network of contacts. This is demonstrated by the scale and scope of my work as a reviewer, my innovative work as Chair of the Membership Involvement Committee of the International Management Division of the Academy of Management, and my academic web site, which is regarded as a major resource site for the research community in the area of International and Cross-Cultural Management (see above).

A. REFEREE AND REVIEW ACTIVITIES

- Departmental Editor Culture and Cognition for *Journal of International Business Studies*
- Area Editor Strategy for the *Australian Journal of Management*
- Associate Editor for *International Journal of Cross-cultural Management*
- Consulting Editor for *The International Journal of Management Reviews*
- Editorial Board member for *International Business Review, European Journal of Management, European Management Review, Human Resource Management* and the newly established *European Journal of International Management*.
- Guest editor for a special issue on International HRM of *In-, door- en uitstroom van personeel*. (1998)
- Co-author of a monthly column "Uit de Ivoren Toren" in *Personeelbeleid*, professional journal of the NVP (Dutch Association for Personnel Management). (1995-1996)
- Regular reviewer for: *Management International Review, Organization Studies, Journal of World Business* and the yearly conferences of the *Academy of International Business, Academy of Management* and the *European International Business Academy*
- Occasional reviewer for:

Academy of Management Journal	*Journal of International Management*
Academy of Management Review	*Journal of Management Studies*
Asia Pacific Journal of HRM	*Management Learning*
Employee Relations	*Personnel Review*
International Journal of HRM	*Thunderbird International Business Review*
International Studies of Management and Organisation	

- Reviewed manuscripts and book proposals for Financial Times Management, Blackwell, Routledge, Sage Publications, Wiley and Prentice Hall.
- Reviewed grant applications for ARC, NWO and ESRC (the Dutch and British equivalents to the Australian Research Council).

B. CHAIR OF THE MEMBERSHIP INVOLVEMENT COMMITTEE (MIC)

From 2001-2003, I was Chair of the newly established Membership Involvement Committee (MIC) of the Intl. Management Division (IMD) of the Academy of Management. The MIC was established to assist the IMD Executive Council in identifying and addressing issues regarding member relations and involvement. I was invited to become Chair because of my broad international network of contacts.

Since barriers for active participation in the Academy are often higher for non-US members, I recruited nearly 50 country representatives, covering more than 40 countries, to help in the running of the MIC. These country representatives acted as a liaison between academics in their own country and myself as Chair of the MIC. To facilitate interaction with IMD members, short bios and pictures of all country reps were included on my web

17

site. Information about activities of the MIC was distributed via the IMD mailings list and newsletter (I wrote a report for each newsletter) and via www.harzing.com.

In addition to regular communication about internationalisation issues with the IMD Executive Committee, I developed a number of initiatives in my role of MIC chair. First, since professional development workshops are an important way to involve members in the division, I organised a PDW on "Doing International Research" for the 2002 Academy meeting. This PDW included presenters from five different countries. Second, I organised an evening at the yearly meeting to introduce new and international members to the Academy. This evening consisted of three parts: a reception, a "roadmap to the Academy" and a "take-a-member-of the-Executive-to-dinner". This has since become a regular part of the IMD conference program.

Based on my work in the IM Division I was recently asked to become the (first non-American) Chair of the Academy of Management Membership Committee. Unfortunately, I had to decline this request, as I could not commit to attending the AoM meeting every year for the next three years.

CONCLUDING SUMMARY

This report has shown that my contribution to the advancement of the discipline is consistent with the criterion for promotion to Level E by achieving and maintaining exceptional distinction in my discipline. In particular, I have shown that my research programs have already made a very significant impact on the field, and that their impact can be expected to increase significantly in the coming years.

My publications have appeared in all major International Business Journals (*Journal of International Business Studies, Management International Review, Journal of World Business, International Business Review* and *Journal of International Management*) as well in top journals in the fields of Strategic Management (*Strategic Management Journal*), Human Resource Management (*Human Resource Management*), Organisation Studies (*Organization Studies*) Organisational Behaviour (*Journal of Organizational Behavior*), Marketing (*Industrial Marketing Management*) and Industrial Relations (*European Journal of Industrial Relations*). These are all journals with very high impact scores and with the exception of one first-authored paper all publications in these journals were single-authored.

To date, I have produced a total of 34 refereed journal articles published/in press (16 of which are single-authored, with another 8 first-authored), one research monograph, two edited research-based textbooks – in which I also wrote six chapters – eight book chapters, and nearly fifty refereed conference papers at high level international conferences. A substantial number of further publications will follow over the next few years. The total number of citations to my work listed in the SSCI (289) and Google Scholar (658), my h-index and the number of recent citations to my work are all evidence of the very strong academic impact of my work.

Since joining the University of Melbourne I have secured one competitive University and two competitive Faculty Grants. In 2004 I was also awarded $185,000 in ARC Discovery Grant funding for a 3-year research project, where I am the only Chief Investigator. This was the **largest** ARC discovery grant awarded to a sole Chief Investigator for a project in the subject area of Management since 2002 (no data available before that time). I received 98% of the funding I requested, which is unique as the normal average funding level lies around 70% and for management projects is usually even lower. I also received funding for a 50% relief of duties, which is hardly ever awarded.

I play very significant leadership roles in international research projects and other collaborations, and have a strong international network and an outstanding academic reputation. Moreover, I generously share my experience with PhD students and junior colleagues from all over the world, displaying a level of research mentoring consistent with that of a senior academic at a research institution of high international standing. I have also shown that I am an active and inspiring teacher and have taken every opportunity to be of service to my department, faculty and the university as a whole. Finally, my service to the discipline was shown to be of a high level. I therefore consider that I have met and exceeded the requirements for promotion to Level E.

18